SAUNDERS PHYSICAL ACTIVITIES SERIES

Edited by

MARYHELEN VANNIER, Ed.D.

Professor and Director, Women's Division
Department of Health and Physical Education
Southern Methodist University

and

HOLLIS F. FAIT, Ph.D.

Professor of Physical Education
School of Physical Education
University of Connecticut

TRACK AND FIELD FOR COLLEGE MEN

ROBERT E. KENNEDY

Head Coach of Track
University of Connecticut
Storrs, Connecticut

ILLUSTRATED BY JAMES BONNER

W. B. SAUNDERS COMPANY
PHILADELPHIA • LONDON • TORONTO

W. B. Saunders Company: West Washington Square
Philadelphia, Pa. 19105

12 Dyott Street
London, WC1A 1DB

1835 Yonge Street
Toronto 7, Ontario

Saunders Physical Activities Series

Track and Field for College Men   SBN 0-7216-5384-7

Print No.   9   8   7   6   5   4   3   2

CONTENTS

CHAPTER 1

INTRODUCTION TO TRACK AND FIELD

Track and field events similar to those in which we participate today date back to the time of the early Greeks. Undoubtedly, fore-runners of these contests were held by man from earliest time, but the first records of formal competition in track and field events were made by the ancient Greeks. A foot race estimated to have been about 200 yards in length was held in the first recorded Olympic Games in 776 B.C. The discus and javelin throws are of Greek origin, and are known to have been prominent events at the funeral games of the Homeric Age. The broad jump event is also thought to have been introduced by the Greeks; the first evidence of it as a contest is its inclusion in the Olympic Games of the Golden Age of Greece.

Other events originated at an early date with other peoples. The Celts apparently began the shot put event. The Irish are reputed to have been the first to engage in a form of pole vaulting.

MODERN TRACK AND FIELD

Modern track and field activities for men are divided into three major groups: running, jumping, and throwing. The running events consist of sprinting, middle distance, distance, and relays. The throwing events consist of the shot put, hammer, discus, and javelin. The jumping events are the long jump, the high jump, and the triple jump. The hurdle events and the pole vault are neither strictly running or jumping, and therefore fall into a category somewhere between the major divisions of track and field activities.

ORGANIZATION OF COMPETITION

In the United States, the formal organization of track and field contests is generally based on a progression of steps. The first step is dual competition, or competition between recognized organizations having restricting regulations. Among these are schools and clubs that compete against one another under strict rules regulating age, ability, and geographic area. Next in the progression is conference competition, usually limited to schools within a geographic range of a few hundred miles. The next step is the national level, and the final step is the world class level, which includes such international competitions as the Olympic Games. Generally, each level of competition has its own records, rules, limitations, and minimum standards for entry into competition. Usually the restrictions at each level have been determined by the desire to improve competition among athletes and for the protection of competitors.

For the more informal contests of intramural or inter-class competition, the regulations are less rigid. Nevertheless, they must be sufficiently restrictive to insure the safety of the participants.

THE PLAYING FIELD

The playing field for track and field competition can best be described as two half-circles, connected by straightaways. The half-circles usually have a radius of more than 100 feet, however, they may be smaller. Generally speaking, tracks are 440 yards per lap and should accommodate a minimum of six lanes, each 42 inches in width, around the track and six or eight lanes of 42 inches on the straightaway. Most modern track surfaces are made of synthetic composition similar to rubber; however, some of the best tracks in the world are still constructed of cinder and/or clay.

The space within the oval track is usually planned to provide areas for all field events. Usually, the long jump, pole vault, and triple jump runways and pits are located along the straightaway sides of the track. The shot put and high jump areas are located within the curved ends of the track, and the discus and javelin areas are located in the mid-field area. In recent years it has become common practice to place the hammer, discus, and javelin throw areas outside the oval, removed from the general spectator and participation area of the infield. The distances now being recorded make these events dangerous within the limited confines of the track. Among the most recent developments in track construction are synthetic infields providing surfaces that are similar to grass, but that are in many respects more efficient for year-round use and less difficult to maintain than grass.

CHAPTER 2

CONDITIONING

Conditioning for track and field is a process of bringing about physiological changes in the body that will improve potential for successful performance. The degree of your success will be related to the quality of your effort.

If you are interested in track and field as a recreational activity, a short period of conditioning each day will provide the necessary physiological changes to protect you against strains and sprains. However, if you aspire to success as a competitor, a greater part of your training must be devoted to conditioning exercises in various forms.

Conditioning exercises, if well selected, will by their very nature improve the quality of your performance in any activity. In most cases, great satisfaction can be gained from these activities because they provide an opportunity to record a measurable improvement during a short period. Increases in strength are quickly noticeable. During weight training sessions you will find that the amount of weight you can lift or the number of times you can lift a particular weight will increase. From day to day, you can detect increased range of movement. On Monday, you can touch your knees; on Tuesday, your ankles; and on Wednesday, your toes. When you begin running, your first run around the track comes hard. As your body condition begins to improve, each run becomes less difficult.

No single factor will contribute more to your success as an athlete than conditioning. Each step in your conditioning program will increase your capacity to do work more efficiently.

CATEGORIES OF CONDITIONING

Conditioning can be divided into three categories: pre-season, early season, and competitive season. These categories can be further divided into many phases: warm-up, individual work, group work, distance work, speed work, weight lifting, warm-down. Each phase is designed to meet a particular need within a category. As in the construction of a pyramid, you will begin with a broad base and build to a fine point of condition. Then, and only then, will you be ready for a maximum effort.

If your primary interest is recreational track and field, you will be most concerned with phase conditioning. You will not be concerned with planning a program for the three seasons of conditioning. You should begin any workout with a period of warm-up. Following this you can engage in one of the other phases. Finally, you should conclude each practice with a warm-down period.

If you are planning a more concentrated approach, you should engage in each of the three categories of training, and your phase training must be planned in relation to your particular needs in the total training program. Each day of practice must include a warm-up period, the inclusion of one or more other forms of phase training, and a warm-down period. This process will begin with the first day of pre-season training and continue until your competitive season has ended.

Warm-up

Your warm-up should consist of easy exercise and light running at the beginning. As your body warms to the exercise, you should increase both the tempo and severity of the exercise until you are completely prepared for the planned effort of the day. The key to a proper warm-up lies in a logical progression from easy activity for all possible muscles to a condition wherein your entire body has been subject to an effort only slightly less than your planned maximum effort for the day. Most athletes tend not to warm-up sufficiently. They feel that hard breathing is an indication that they are properly warmed. At the end of a warm-up period you should be perspiring freely. Your joints should have been extended progressively to their limits and your breathing should be hard. During practice, if the length of your warm-up is too long, no great harm will result. You may find that you must reduce the length of your planned work or the severity of the work. In competition, if the length or severity of your warm-up is too great, it will probably result in an effort less than your potential best. Learn from practice when you have warmed-up enough.

Individual work

Individual work is a form of training during which you practice the basic skills of your event. You must enter each of these sessions with a definite plan, and you should move from the most simple to the most complex movements of the event. Repeat the basic skills again and again until they become natural movements to you. Whenever possible, have a partner who can work as an observer and discuss your movements with him. When you engage in individual work, you must concentrate on proper execution of the fundamental movements.

Group work

Group work is a form of training during which a number of athletes practice the same skills together. If you have a coach, group work will almost always be under his direction. Without a coach, one member of the group should attempt to serve as observer and discussion leader as you consider the efforts of each athlete. During group work sessions, you have an opportunity to develop individual skills as you compare your ability with other competitors in the same event.

Distance work

Distance work training is a form usually reserved for runners. It is important that all runners engage in some degree of distance running, since it develops muscular endurance. The advantage to runners is obvious, but field event men also benefit from distance running. The longer a field man is free from fatigue, the greater and more consistent his effort will normally be. For sprint event men, the positive value of distance training comes in developing the ability to sustain their maximum effort for a longer period of time.

Speed work

Speed work is an important form of training for all track and field events. In the final analysis, whether you are a runner or a field event man, how fast you propel the implement or your body will in some way be the measure of your success. The amount of speed work in which you engage should be carefully controlled. During any maximum effort you subject your body to great stress and strain; the danger of injury is increased and the development of fatigue is rapid. During speed training it is usually advisable to stop whenever a repeated breakdown in form begins to occur, since this is an indication that your muscles have ceased to function in their trained pattern of movements. Generally, fatigue will be the cause of the breakdown.

Weight lifting

A good weight lifting program will develop the strength required to execute the skills of your event more efficiently. As you improve your physical strength, you will be able to practice for longer periods.

At the same time, you will enhance your capacity for normal daily physical routines, and therefore arrive at practice better prepared for the physical workout related to your event.

Weight lifting must be regulated both in effort and in duration. Failure to provide enough rest after periods of weight lifting will result in fatigue build-up that will prevent the desired muscle reaction in strength or endurance. Before you begin weight lifting, gain some knowledge of the muscle groups you are attempting to develop. Equally important, gain some knowledge regarding strength and endurance development.

Warm-down

During a practice session, your body has been working close to, or at, capacity. When you have completed your workout, it is recommended that you take the time to bring your body functions back to normal. To do this, engage in light recovery activities: easy running, light exercise, and finally walking until you feel you have recovered from your efforts.

Pre-season conditioning

If you aspire to be a great athlete, your daily program will include almost all parts of phase training. However, each part will serve as a unit of a master plan to bring about more complete physical development.

The pre-season period is devoted first to general body conditioning and then to a broad program of fundamental training for your event. You will spend considerable time in easy running periods if you are preparing for the races. If you are planning to compete in the field events, you will spend some time in running training and the remainder in developing coordinated movements related to your event.

During this period, you will increase the range of muscular movement and decrease the resistance of antagonistic muscles through stretching exercises and practice. Your primary goal will be total conditioning, and your secondary goal will be development of fundamental skills and movement.

You may experience some degree of muscular tenderness during this part of your training program. However, continued adherence to your daily routine will quickly minimize this discomfort. Great restraint must be exercised during your pre-season conditioning program. The temptation to run, to jump, or to throw too far before you are ready can result in injury that will hamper your normal program.

Early season conditioning

The early season conditioning period extends from that time when your body has attained a fair degree of conditioning until you are engaged in the competitive part of your program.

During this part of your program, you will engage in the bulk of your hard training. You must divide your weekly program into periods of event training, hard conditioning, and weight lifting. You must move from the fundamental training technique to the advanced training technique. You must, in effect, put the final touches on your skill development.

If you are a runner, you must devote your time to repeated training runs selected to improve your capabilities in your event. You must practice running distances greater than your race distance in order to develop added strength, and distances less than your race distance in order to develop speed.

If you are a field event man, you must devote your time to final improvements of your techniques. You must prepare a format from which to operate during competition. You must engage in periods of exact technique movement and periods of maximum effort during which you attempt to attain exact technique. Each day must have a goal of technique, distance, or strength improvement.

For this period of training you must develop well-planned routines. Each day must be part of a progression toward improvement. Your warm-up period should be studied for indications of when you are ready for serious work. Your drills should become successively more intense and strenuous. You are, in effect, narrowing toward the top of the pyramid, preparing for the "big effort."

Competitive Conditioning

The competitive conditioning period is the most critical in your entire program. Over the months you have prepared for the short competitive period during which your body should be at maximum efficiency. You will be required to work hard during competition, but you will not engage in long strenuous conditioning periods between competitions. You cannot cease to practice, yet you cannot afford to expend energy that you will need for competition. Skill practice must continue, and you must attempt to correct mistakes that may have been made during your most recent competitive effort. On the other hand, you must limit the strenuousness of your workouts.

If your program has been selected properly, your primary problem at this stage in the conditioning program will be to maintain a "keen edge" for competition. The number of competitions in which you engage should be carefully selected on the basis of available time for practice and competition.

When your competitive season has ended, taper off. Engage in other activities related or unrelated to track and field. Enjoy the fine physical condition your training has given you and have fun in your activity. If your experience has been a good one, and you take time to get away from track and field for a while, you will return the next year with a fresh eager outlook on the season to come. You will be a trackman.

Special Training Methods

There are many methods of training that may be suggested or scheduled for you during your training periods. The method of training and the degree of intensity will depend on your condition and need at the time.

Cross-country

This method of training can be the least strenuous of the forms to be considered, or it can be performed on a more difficult level. It consists of continuous running over natural land contours. It can be graded in degree of severity by faster running or by covering again and again the most difficult land contours.

Easy cross-country running is ideal for preparing for the more vigorous training of your early season program. Usually, two or three days of cross-country running during the pre-season training will help you develop strength and endurance. The distance you run in training should be related to the distance you are planning to run in competition. The greater the distance you plan to run in competition, the greater will be the distance you run in cross-country training.

Fartlek

This method of training affords the opportunity for more strenuous training. However, it has its limitations because training usually occurs over rough, uneven ground, where it is hard to generate great speed. Fartlek, meaning "speed play," calls for running variable speeds and distances as you feel the need or urge to run them.

During fartlek training, vary your work from short, fast runs to long runs both hard and easy, of one-half mile or more. Between each of the more intense runs, jog at a recovery pace. When you feel the desire to change tempo, do so. When you are in a group, you may alternate the leadership in order to have a more varied tempo. However, you as the runner must work at the fartlek program. When you are at jogging tempo, run easily; when you change tempo, make a complete change and move fast.

Interval running

During interval training, you will run continuous changes of pace at fixed times and over fixed distances. This form of running can be restricted to the track, or it can be run over established parts of a cross-country course. If run over a cross-country course, you must attempt to find smooth areas where you can run at high speed without fear of leg injury from rough terrain. During interval training, a fast run is followed by a slow recovery jog. For example, you may run a 220 at 30 seconds, followed by a 220 at 90 seconds. You may repeat this process 15 times. The distance run may be varied on different days, and the period of jogging may be reduced or lengthened in relation to the distance run. However, you must attempt to complete the planned interval workout each time. If necessary, the 15 repetitions of the 220 may be divided into sets of three or five runs with a short recovery rest between each set.

The primary purpose during an interval workout is to increase cardiovascular efficiency. Later in the training period, emphasis can be placed on speed. Repeated runs of short distances are also useful in developing a good sense of pace, so interval training can serve this purpose as well.

Repetition running

This method of training is the most strenuous of all. It consists of repeatedly running distances less than your competitive event at slower than race pace speed. Between runs, your body is given time to recover sufficiently to run the next unit. For example, you may repeatedly run three-quarters of your total race distance. Your pace must be slower and your body must be rested after each effort. Repetitions may be run at faster than race speed, but if they are, the distance run must be reduced to about one-half your total race distance. Repetition workouts are long, hard, and demanding. They should be put off until you have attained a high degree of conditioning.

Time trials

Another method of training is the time trial. Usually this form of training is reserved for the competitive season when the period between competitions is too long to maintain top condition. Most time trials are run at distances slightly shorter than race distance. They require a maximum effort on your part and are rarely repeated on the same day. Time trials serve two purposes: they provide a method for measuring your potential and they serve as a rehearsal for actual competition.

Weight lifting

This form of training is considered by all coaches as an integral part of track and field conditioning. Increased strength will lead to improved performance, and the quality and quantity of your weight training will usually be related to the quality of your competitive effort.

Weight training should be progressive. It should be initiated well within your capacity and increased in constant stages. When you begin weight lifting, start with light weights; at the end of a given period increase the amount of weight. Increase the amount of weight regularly.

The concept of weight training progress can be generalized to some degree by the following statement: Muscular strength will be developed by lifting near maximum capacity on sets of low repetition count. Muscular endurance will be developed by lifting relatively light weights in sets of high repetition count. Strength is developed through an overload program. Endurance is developed through a repetition program.

CHAPTER 3

SPRINTING

It is often said that sprinters are born, not made. Yet history has never recorded an incident in which an untrained athlete has stepped onto a track and established a new world record. Good sprinting is the product of long hours of training. It differs from other forms of running in many ways. The most obvious differences come in the speed of leg action, the force of leg action against the ground, and the length of stride. There are two basic sprint events: the 100 yard run and the 220 yard run. The sprint races can be divided, generally, into three parts: the start, the run, and the finish.

THE START

All sprint races are initiated from behind a line drawn at right angles to the boundaries of the track. Three commands are given at the start. They are: "Runners, go to your marks," "Set," and "Go." These commands are spaced so that the runners can execute the motions related to the commands in a relaxed fashion.

Starting blocks

During the early development of sprinting, most runners dug small holes in the surface of the track, into which they placed the ball of each foot and the toes. These so-called "starting holes" were effective aids to overcoming inertia at the start of the race; however, they resulted in considerable damage to the surface of the starting area. The rules of track now provide for the use of starting blocks in the starting area.

A starting block is a wooden or metal device that is pinned or nailed to the surface of the track and is used to assist the sprinter in attaining a more efficient start while not damaging the area. The starting block consists of two adjustable platforms that provide resistance to the feet at the start of the race. When using the blocks, the rules provide that some part of each foot must be in contact with the track surface.

11

The starting positions

Effective placement of the hands and feet in the starting positions is the prime consideration. Starting positions are described in three terms that, in general, refer to the relative positioning of both hands and feet. They are: the bunched start, the medium start, and the elongated start.

In all sprint starting positions the hands are placed on the track with the thumb and index finger parallel to and behind the starting line. The feet are placed a comfortable distance apart with one foot ahead of the other.

In the bunched start, the distance from the hands to the front foot is greatest, and the distance from the front foot to the rear foot is shortest. Most of the weight is distributed over the front foot, so that it is the prime mover of the body. Sprinters with powerful legs have successfully used this start.

In the elongated start, the distance from the hands to the front foot is shortest, and the distance from the front foot to the rear foot is greatest. The rear leg becomes the prime mover of body in this start, and a slight delay is experienced as the weight moves to the front foot.

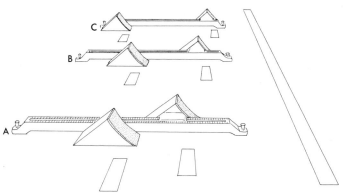

Relative positioning of starting blocks in bunch (A), medium (B), and elongated (C), placement.

In the medium start, the spacing between the hands and the front foot and between the front foot and the rear foot is more equal. The weight is distributed more evenly over the four points of contact with the track and the runner achieves more powerful thrust.

With experience, block spacing will usually become an individual choice, based to a great degree on physical characteristics and the results obtained in competition. Since the medium start seems to prove most effective for the average individual, it is the one that will be presented here.

Try these positions for the medium start: Locate the front block 15 to 18 inches behind the starting line. Locate the rear block another 16 to 20 inches behind the front block. In this position, the knee of your rear leg and the toes of your front foot will be approximately in line.

To take the starting position, stand in front of your blocks. Place your hands on the track in the general area of the starting line, and back your feet into the blocks. In a race, this is the position you would take on the command, "Runners, go to your marks." As you back each foot into the blocks, test them by exerting pressure to the rear. Be sure that they are firmly set.

Sprinter in medium start positioning.

Next, locate your hands behind the starting line in the prescribed manner with your thumb and index fingers parallel to the line. Place the knee of your rear leg on the ground. Relax your neck muscles slightly, and focus your eyes about three feet forward of the starting line. Roll your hips forward and up until your back is slightly higher than your head. This is the position you would take on the command, "Set." In this position, your arms and hands are supporting

Sprinter in "set" positioning.

part of your body weight. The amount of weight supported will be related in part to the relative position of your feet. A partner can be very useful at this time. Standing away to your side, he can observe the position of your legs. Your front leg should be bent slightly less than 90° and your rear leg bent slightly in excess of 90°. If they are not, he can suggest the necessary adjustments of either the block placement or your body position.

Once you have moved to the set position, you must remain motionless until the gun is fired. Do not attempt to look down the track when you are in the set position. Raising your head will cause your neck muscles to tighten and will result in restricted breathing. It might also produce an undesired upward thrust when the gun is fired. Your eyes should continue to focus on the same spot selected for the "Go to your mark" position.

In competition, you will be held in this "set" position for about two seconds. During this period you should concentrate on execution of the starting movements when the gun fires.

At the sound of the gun, drive forward out of the blocks. The arm nearest to the front foot swings forward and up in a short uppercut motion as the rear leg drives forcefully against the block, producing forward thrust. The arm nearer to the rear foot swings back and up in a flexed position. Both arms should be flexed at 90° and should be swung with only enough force to counter the action of the leg movement.

Sprinter leaving blocks on first step.

If your movements are coordinated, your arms will reverse their direction of swing just as your rear foot strikes the track and your front foot pushes off the block. The length of your first stride will depend on your power and speed. It must definitely fall beyond the starting line, and in most cases should be from 8 to 12 inches beyond the starting line. Do not attempt to make your first step short. Your problem is to move down the track as fast as possible.

As you push out of the starting blocks, the angle of your body will be related to your speed. The faster you leave the blocks, the more acute will be the angle of your body. When you are moving out of the starting blocks, body lean is the effect of high speed and not the cause of it. As your skill and speed improve, your body angle or lean will increase and should, therefore, not be of great concern at this stage of your training.

THE RUN

After you have left the starting blocks, each stride becomes increasingly longer. Concentrate on high knee lift and on "stroking the ground back under your foot" as your foot touches the ground. High knee lift will produce a more rapid fall of your foot toward the track, resulting in increased leg speed. As you gain speed, your body will become progressively more erect until you are moving at top speed. Now, the degree of your body lean will be only as much as is needed to overcome wind resistance.

Sprinter in full stride.

The length of your stride will depend on the speed you attain. The faster you move, the greater will be the distance between each contact of your foot with the track. Many beginning runners believe a sprinter runs with a short stride because leg action is so fast and contact with the ground is so short. In fact, the sprinter's stride is usually the longest of all runners.

During the running phase of the sprint races, you must concentrate on action to the exclusion of all other things. Do not think of your opponent. Run from start to finish, concentrating on speed and coordination. In the 100 yard run, maintain the speed you develop for the longest possible period. Training will help you develop the ability to relax as you run at high speed. In this case, relaxed running means the lack of opposition from antagonistic muscles, or muscles that will produce resistance to the free movement of those being used to run.

THE FINISH

The last few yards of a race can be the most critical stage in the entire distance. As fatigue begins to develop, running efficiency is hampered and body control and coordination can be lost. Between 75 and 85 yards from the start, you will attain your greatest possible speed. Attempt to maintain this speed to a point 10 yards beyond the finish line. Do not stop running the instant you cross the finish line. Poor judgment may cause you to slow too quickly, and a sudden stop can cause severe injury to your leg muscles. Do not lunge for the finish line. Run past it with the best possible form.

THE 100 YARD RUN

The 100 yard run is a full-out run for the entire distance. From the sound of the gun you must attempt to continue to accelerate over the entire course. Because of the short duration of the race, breathing is no problem. Do not attempt to force your breathing, since it will usually result in some degree of muscle tension in the shoulder or chest area. Physiologically, a single breath is more than sufficient to complete the race.

In competition, before your race has been called, you should have completed any equipment or uniform adjustments, ascertained your running lane, and completed your warm-up exercises. When you are called to the starting line, you adjust and locate your starting blocks and then stand in your lane until ordered by the starter to remove your warm-up uniform. If there is a delay in the start, jog or run in your lane, but do not leave the track without permission from the starter.

When the first command is given, begin the same routine you have practiced throughout your training. When the gun is fired, begin your acceleration, remain in your lane through the entire race, and after you have crossed the finish line return in your lane back to the finish line.

THE 220 YARD RUN

The 220 yard run differs from the 100 yard run in one important aspect. It is impossible to run the total distance at maximum speed. Therefore, you must "float" for part of the race. The start of the 220 yard run is exactly like that in the 100 yard run. However, about 60 to 70 yards from the starting line, the float begins.

The float

During this stage of the run, concentrate on relaxation, which will maintain your speed with the least expenditure of energy. Some runners find it helpful to think that they are running downhill. Speed is maintained, but energy is conserved. This stage of the race demands efficiency in running. High knee lift and coordinated arm action are extremely important to maximum efficiency in stride and leg speed.

Without the float, fatigue would cause your muscles to tire and become inefficient. You would reach the critical stage in the race and be unable to produce a strong finish. The duration of the float is about 100 to 120 yards. Then you must attempt to gather your strength for the final drive past the finish line.

Only experience will teach you how long you should float and when you can drive for the finish line. Beginning too early or too late can be equally critical errors. When you are running the 220, concentrate on how well you are executing the various parts of the race. Remember for the future what experience of the past has taught you.

PRACTICE SESSIONS

Sprinting practice sessions must be very detailed. At various times they must include: starting practice, high speed running, floating practice, finishing drive, and endurance running. Although the 100 yard run is considered a speed race, the runner with the greatest endurance will win, if all other factors are equal.

When you have attained good physical condition and are prepared to begin hard sprinting, break your practice sessions into units. The amount of time you spend on a unit will depend on your particular need, and the order in which you practice or develop each unit may vary, but all parts of a proper program must be included.

Your first unit could be concerned with starting. You could begin by experimenting with block placement and body position. Locate the starting blocks on the track in a medium start position. Have a partner stand to your side and attempt to adjust your body to the proper position as he gives you the starting commands. When you feel you are comfortable in the set position, think about the movements that should occur. Execute them in a slow, controlled rhythm. Concentrate on coordination and do not attempt to develop speed. Repeat the process until you feel you can add speed and still maintain control. After a series of 10 or 12 starts, move to another activity. With your partner, try striding as fast as possible with the least expenditure of energy.

Your second unit can be used for endurance running. Go out on the cross-country course and run for 20 to 30 minutes without stopping. Do not attempt to run too fast, but try not to stop. Return to the track and rest until you feel reasonably refreshed. Run for a distance of 30 to 40 yards, increasing your speed constantly until you feel you are at maximum. Maintain maximum speed for 20 to 30 yards and slow gradually. Repeat this practice until you tire.

Your third unit can be used to practice high knee lift. Begin running at a slow pace. Lift your knees higher and higher. While executing this movement, attempt to pull your foot to the rear as it is about to strike the ground. Your foot must contact the ground under your center of gravity if you are to develop good high speed running technique. Work for arm and leg coordination and body balance.

Your fifth unit can be used to develop the start and acceleration away from the blocks. Attempt to develop powerful arm movement to balance the thrust of your legs. Before you attain what you feel is your top speed, float for 20 to 30 yards and slow to a stop.

Whenever possible, practice sprinting with a partner, but don't concern yourself with his movements. Concentrate entirely on what you are doing and how you can improve on it.

Good sprinting techniques are developed as a result of repeated high speed runs. You cannot hope to become a sprinter without hard training.

COUNTDOWN

When you are finally prepared to compete, have a set of quick review questions ready to answer in the final moments before the race begins.

1. Are my starting blocks properly adjusted?
2. On the "set" command, where should my hips be located?
3. Where should my eyes be focused when the gun fires?
4. What is the sequence of coordinated moves when I start?
5. Should I watch any other runner in the field?
6. When the gun fires, should I think, or should I move with the sound?

SAFETY PRECAUTIONS

Sprinting would seem to involve little danger. However, considerable care should be exercised to avoid injury. Your shoes must be properly cared for to avoid a tear or broken lace under the great strain of sprinting. Worn spikes can cause serious injury if they permit slipping on the running surface. You must remain in your lane at all times to avoid the danger of being spiked or bumped while running. Never stop quickly for fear of muscle injury. When a race is completed, never run to another competitor to wish him well. There is the danger that you might step on his foot or spike his leg because you are overexcited. Don't wear spikes on any surface other than the track.

CHAPTER 4

MIDDLE DISTANCE

The basic requirements for the middle distance events are speed and endurance. The distances run in these events are 440 yards and 880 yards. Because of the speed at which it is now run, the 440 event is considered a long sprint; however, it still remains in the middle distance class for all but the most accomplished runners. The 440 and 880 runs are the backbone of all track teams. A team with strong middle distance runners will generally be a strong team, because the runners are able to perform well in the sprints, relay, and mile run, along with the middle distance events.

THE START

There are two basic starts in the middle distance races: the sprint start, which is described in the chapter on sprinting, and the standing start.

The standing start

This form of start is usually reserved for the 880 yard run, but it has been effectively used for the 440 yard run. Although it is slightly less efficient than the sprint start, there is less energy consumed in the standing start. Therefore, if well executed, the loss of time or distance that may be entailed will be compensated for at the end of the race by the energy saved. If the race is to be started from a common starting line, the standing start usually proves more effective, since there is less danger of being bumped off-balance by another runner. A runner starting from the sprint start position can easily be knocked off-balance during the first few steps of the start. Experimentation will teach you which of the two starts is most effective for you.

For the standing start, stand with your toes behind the starting line and both feet pointed in the direction you will run. Move your left foot about 18 inches to the rear. Now, bend both knees and permit the greater part of your body weight to be supported by your front

Middle distance runner in standing start position.

leg and foot. Your left arm should be placed forward in the normal running position and your right arm to the rear in a counterbalance position. Next, incline your chest toward the running surface until you feel you are about to lose balance.

While the starting commands are being given, you must maintain this position. At the sound of the gun, your rear foot pushes your weight forward and your front leg then begins to thrust hard against the track. This leg action should be balanced by an equally strong action of the opposite arm in order to provide coordinated rhythm.

The most common error in this form of start is permitting your weight to drop back to your rear foot at the sound of the gun. Your weight must move forward with the sound of the gun, and your rear foot must step onto the running surface at least two or three feet down the track. High knee action of your rear leg will facilitate a good first stride.

STRIDE DEVELOPMENT

A stride is the distance covered between two successive steps. Successful middle distance running requires the development of well-executed and coordinated strides. The middle distance stride can best be described as a high-speed, energy-saving leg movement designed to carry the runner the greatest possible distance between each foot placement with the least expenditure of energy. Stride development is the result of training. The length of your stride will be the product of your leg speed and strength. While both these factors are related, the latter can be developed to a high degree, while the former is considered more a hereditary characteristic.

Leg strength produces the force of leg action against the ground. The harder your leg pushes against the ground, the greater will be the resulting movement of your body over the ground. It follows, then, that conditioning your legs through weight training will produce more desirable stride characteristics.

Leg speed can be improved through repeated runs at a pace faster than race pace. As your legs are conditioned to running at faster paces, you will be able to run at a slightly slower pace with more relaxed control. As you improve this ability, you will find that your stride will improve. While your leg speed carries you over the ground with faster movements, your leg strength will carry you farther during each stride. The two factors working in combination will permit you a more efficient middle distance stride.

The duration of the stride period of an 880 race is greater than in the 440 race, and therefore requires considerably more training in technique. While sprinting calls for running on the balls of your feet, striding requires a different foot placement. A single stride begins when the ball of your foot breaks contact with the ground. Your lead knee lifts to about half-way between belt level and the ground and the lower half of your leg moves forward to a complete extension. The lower half of your leg begins to flex backward and you land on the ball of your foot, slightly forward of your center of gravity. The heel of your foot then settles gently onto the ground as your weight passes over the foot. The heel now lifts off the ground and, as your opposite knee begins to lift, you execute a complete extension of the leg now in the rear. This method is referred to as the ball-heel-ball action and permits an immediate shift to sprinting form through a slightly higher knee lift and a more forceful rearward stroke of the lead leg.

THE 440 YARD RUN

The 440 yard run usually covers two turns or one full lap of the track. It may be initiated from a common starting line, or from a staggered start. When run from a common starting line, all runners take a position along a line across the mid-point of the straightaway. When a staggered start is used, all runners start in separate lanes and remain in those lanes at all times. Although the positions of the runners are staggered, the distance in each lane is equated with every other lane. The runner in the inside lane, or pole position, appears to be starting behind all other runners. However, each runner in the lanes to his outside is running a greater turn radius; he is therefore positioned ahead of the pole runner at the start of the race.

Lane running requires great skill, since you cannot be sure of the relative position of other runners until the last few yards of your race. The closer a runner is to the pole position, the greater his advantage in knowing the approximate position of other runners, but the outside lane runners dare not look back to locate their opponents for fear of running out of their lane while they look about. A race to be run in lanes must be planned in advance and run according to plan.

Three factors will usually influence your race plan. They are: your potential ability, your position relative to the best runner in the field, and your position relative to the pole lane. If you are the best runner in the field, your position relative to the pole will be the only important factor. If you are on or near the pole lane, you will be able to observe most of the runners and you will be able to run your race in relation to their progress. If you are in an outside lane, your best plan will usually be to run the early part of the race at a fast pace in order to gain a psychological advantage over your opponents. If you have an apparently long lead near the finish of the race, only the best competitors will challenge your position.

If you are not the best runner in the field, the closer you are to the best runner the more you can draw on his ability to run the race well. Again, if you are positioned in an outside lane, run a fast pace in the early part of the race. Your advantage coming off the last turn may prevent a challenge by other runners.

As you gain experience, your ability to judge pace will serve to permit you to plan a race based on exact timing at various points along the course. You will divide the course into time periods and produce your best effort by attaining given points on a time schedule.

Generally, it is a good policy to get off the starting line fast, and move to the front of the field, or close to it. During the stride phase of your race, you must continue to maintain momentum, and if possible move ahead, or stay close to the lead position.

If your race plan calls for a late sprint, it must be executed with complete confidence from a position close to the lead and it must be timed so as to continue to the finish line. Failure to maintain your finishing drive to the line may result in your being passed by strong finish runners in the last few strides.

If your race is to be run from a common starting line, many factors will influence your race plan. Your position entering the first turn will probably be the most critical factor. If you are leading, you must maintain the lead throughout the turn or you will find yourself in a position from which you cannot move to the outside until there is a break in the line of runners passing you. If you are in a line passing around the pole runner, maintain your position until you arrive on the straightaway. Moving along the straightaway, if you are the leader, try to maintain the lead. If you are unable to, you must at least stay close to any passing runners. If you are a trailing runner, move to the outside in order to be able to pass slower runners without changing your course. As you approach the final turn, you must attempt to gain a position on the pole regardless of your relative location in the field. Running an outside lane increases your total distance run by approximately 7 feet for each lane away from the pole. Before you complete the turn, begin to accelerate toward the finish. This action will assist you in attaining a good position as you move up the straightaway. If you permit other runners to move to the outside of you, they may form a passing line that you will be unable to break into and you will be hopelessly left behind at the critical point in the race. If you are a lead runner on the straightaway, or if you attain the lead after gaining the straightaway, you must maintain a straight line course to the finish line. If you should veer to the inside, or outside, and thereby interfere with another runner, you are subject to disqualification.

As you near the finish line, do not look for the relative position of other runners. Many men who have looked to the left have been passed on the right and vice versa. Run at least 10 yards beyond the finish before you begin to slow your pace to make certain you do not decrease your speed until you are over the finish line.

THE 880 YARD RUN

The 880 yard run usually covers four turns or two full laps of the track. Usually, runners in the 880 race will start from a common starting line.

Since the 880 provides ample time for the development of strategy during the race, it is difficult to attempt a pre-race plan without knowing the normal running habits of all competitors. Even this fact may be of no value if a single competitor changes what might normally be expected of him. Two possible plans may be attempted: (1) You can plan to run at the front of the field for the entire race. In this case, you must have an exact sense of pace in order not to force the race beyond your ability. If another runner passes you, you must continue at your own pace in the belief that you will eventually overcome the leader before the finish line. (2) You can plan to run in the field during most of the race. At some pre-planned point you will begin your sprint for the finish line. If another competitor begins his sprint before you, it will be necessary for you to change plan and move with him. Once you make your move and begin sprinting, you are committed to run at your best speed to the finish line.

When a field of 880 runners of equal capability are competing against one another, the race will often develop into a game of challenge and rechallenge as each runner attempts to use his best ability to force the race in his favor. During your training, you must attempt to learn how you best run this distance through experiments with various paced movements.

PRACTICE SESSIONS

Practice sessions will depend on your individual need. Your training will vary from short sprints, during which you learn to get away from the starting line quickly and build your running speed, to cross-country runs, during which you develop your endurance.

Developing knowledge of your capabilities will be important. If you have basic speed, you must learn how much. If you have basic endurance, you must learn how long and at what pace it will best serve you.

As in all track and field events, middle distance running demands hard work and concentration on a definite purpose. It is not sufficient just to get on the track and run. Each day of work must have a definite purpose and the skills of your event must be learned early in your training. Develop a plan of practice units to give you continuity in your workouts.

Your first unit can concern itself with development of stride. If possible, work with a group of runners and, in effect, practice your skills against them. As you run around the track, attempt to get good ball-heel-ball foot placement. Periodically lengthen or shorten your stride to learn if you run more efficiently in either situation. Attempt to learn good coordination of arms and legs. Learn to change pace quickly and move past another runner before he is aware you have made your move.

Your second unit can concern itself with learning the standing start and how to accelerate quickly from the starting line. Practice the standing and the sprint start until you have mastered the skills to perfection. The advantage of a quick, efficient start can gain you ideal positioning in an important race.

Your third unit can be used to develop a fast change of pace to the final sprinting action used near the finish line. Here you will attempt to increase your knee lift and the force with which your feet strike the ground on each stride. Learn to run behind other competitors and use their closeness to help maintain your speed through mental contact with their movements.

During your fourth unit you can develop a sense of race pace. You can practice running fixed distances at an exact speed. This can be accomplished with the aid of a partner who calls your time as you pass fixed points along the track.

Practice sessions are a means for developing the skills necessary to become a great runner. A middle distance runner's season will be long if he desires to excel. Most great middle distance men begin their training during the cross-country season and continue to the end of the year.

COUNTDOWN

Prior to competing in either of the middle distance races, you will be concerned with various factors. Before you run, ask yourself the questions that will most relate to your competition.

1. Am I properly warmed up?
2. What are my race plan and my alternate plan?
3. How can I get away from the starting line quickly?
4. How can I avoid being caught in a position where I will not be able to run my best race?
5. What pace do I plan for the first half of the race?
6. What do I know about the running habits of my opponents?
7. Who is the most important man in the competition and how can I use his ability to my advantage?

SAFETY PRECAUTIONS

Although it would not seem that there are many safety precautions needed in middle distance running, a few extremely important considerations cannot be overlooked. You must maintain your running shoes in the best possible condition. Your spikes must be kept sharp and at the proper length for the condition of the track. If you develop any sore spots or incur an injury, report it and have it treated immediately. During a race, avoid running close to the curb; stepping on the curb can cause you to trip or fall. Never cut to the inside or outside without having two-stride clearance on another runner.

CHAPTER 5

DISTANCE RUNNING

Most races shorter than 10,000 meters (1 yard = .9144 meters) and longer than 880 yards are considered distance. The form used in distance running will differ with the demands of the race.

At the start of a distance race, you are a sprinter until you have gained momentum. When the pace of the race settles down, your form is not unlike that of a cross-country man. You must run to conserve energy and retain enough strength for the final sprint to the finish line.

Foot placement and arm carriage are the two most important factors to consider in distance running. Once the pace of the race has become constant, your foot is placed on the track with your weight being carried well back near the heel. This placement permits a rolling action from the back of the foot forward. Knee lift is reduced; arm action is minimized and serves primarily to help maintain good balance. Landing toward the rear of the foot reduces stride length, but it permits your legs to relax as your center of gravity passes over the foot on the ground.

THE START

Almost all experienced runners prefer the standing start for distance races because it helps conserve energy. One foot is placed close to the starting line while the other is located about 18 inches to the rear. Your body weight is shifted over the front foot and your arms should be positioned in natural balance position. At the sound of the gun, your rear foot extends quickly and as your weight moves forward your front foot pushes hard against the ground. Your arms must swing forcefully during the early strides until you attain the position you desire in relation to the other runners in the field. Once you have established your position and your momentum is holding you there, you can settle into your distance stride.

THE RUN

During a distance race you should attempt to maintain a constant speed, since adjustments will usually produce excessive fatigue.

If you are running at the front of the field, do not look to the rear at any time. Maintain a straight course and listen for any change in position or pace that might occur to the rear. If you are in second place, maintain a position about one stride to the rear and one-half a body width to the leader's outside. In this position you will be able to get around him with ease if he slows his pace or stumbles. If you are farther to the rear than second, always keep your eyes on the front runner. Doing so will enable you to know when he increases his speed. You can then do likewise. If he moves away from you without your realizing he has gained speed, your chances of catching him are greatly reduced.

Distance runner in proper position for easy pass.

Different fields of runners will cause race strategy to change. If the first half of the race has been slow, the third quarter may suddenly become fast. If the race has been slow through the third quarter, you can almost be sure that each runner is saving his best effort for the final quarter. Knowing your opponents' abilities will dictate how soon or how late you can begin your final sprint.

THE SPRINT

If the early stages of a race have been slow, the final stage will usually be fast. When the pace changes, your style will change with it. During the sprint you will increase the power stroke of your arms and increase the lift of your knees so as to produce a more forceful contact with the track. Your sprint must begin as far as possible from the finish line and it must continue past the line. Any slowing in the last few strides can be dangerous unless you have a commanding lead.

If another runner challenges your position, you must be alert to hear or see him before he is able to generate greater speed.

If the early stages of a race have been fast, it is important to be in a commanding position early in the last quarter. When the early stages of a race have been fast, you can never presume that the pace will slow enough for you to fall behind and then catch up the distance lost. You must go with the pace and rely on your training to keep you with the pace to the finish line.

DISTANCE TRAINING

Distance training will vary with your individual need. Endurance may be improved by running long distances at controlled pace. Speed may be improved through repeated runs of short distance at rapid pace. You should be familiar with the training procedures of both middle distance and cross-country runners. Distance training is a slow, constant process that can be continued year-round if you wish to excel in the sport.

CHAPTER 6

RELAY RACING

Relay races are run at a variety of distances, depending on the particular type of meet or conference wherein the competition occurs. Among the generally recognized relays are: 4 × 110, 4 × 220, 4 × 440, 4 × 880, 4 × 1 mile, the sprint medley (440, 220, 220, 880), the distance medley (440, 880, 1320, 1 mile), and the 4 × 120 shuttle hurdle relay. With the exception of the shuttle hurdle relay, each of these events is run around the circular track and each requires passing a baton from one runner to the next successive runner. In the shuttle hurdle relay, a hand tap is made from one runner to the next.

The relay baton is tubular, 11.81 inches or less in length, its weight is not less than 50 grams, and its circumference is 120 millimeters. During a relay race, it is passed from hand to hand in any manner desired by the four team members. However, the pass of the baton must occur within a 20-meter zone marked on the track at prescribed intervals related to the event.

In the 440 and 880 relays, outgoing runners may position themselves and begin running 10 meters outside the passing zone. The pass of the baton must, however, occur within the legal zone. In all other relays, the runners must position themselves entirely within the passing zone.

In the shuttle hurdle relay, a runner may not leave the starting blocks until he has been tapped by the previous runner, who runs his race in the adjacent lane.

In the sprint relays (440 and 880), the baton pass is extremely critical and requires that the incoming runner catch the outgoing runner to complete the pass. In all other relay races, the responsibility for completing the pass lies with the outgoing runner. He must be sure not to leave his position too soon.

Relay passes are divided into two types: "blind" passes and "sight" passes. Blind passes are usually used in the sprint relays because they provide for an uninterrupted flow of high speed movements. Two methods of "blind" passing are recommended: the right-left-left-right, and the inside left. In the right-left pass, the lead runner carries the baton in his right hand and passes to the next runner's left hand. The second runner continues with the baton in his left hand and passes to the right hand of the next runner. The third runner passes from his right hand to the left hand of the fourth runner. For the inside left pass, the lead runner carries the baton in his left hand and passes to the right hand of the second runner, who immediately switches the baton to his left hand. The second runner passes to the right hand of the third runner who also immediately switches the baton and passes to the right hand of the fourth runner. The fourth runner has no need to switch the baton during his portion of the race.

In the right-left pass there is no switching of the baton by the individual runner, but because of the nature of the pass each man must deliver the baton with almost hand-to-hand contact or there will be nothing remaining for the last runner to grasp. As each pass is completed, the receiver's hand is moving up the baton. The first runner must therefore grasp the baton at the very bottom so as to leave sufficient room for the last man to take his grip. During the 440 relay, where two passes occur on the turn, there appear to be certain advantages in this pass. The lead runner completes his pass running close to the inside edge of the track. The second runner takes the baton in his left hand and completes his run on the outer edge of his lane, passing to the inside edge where the third man is running. The third man takes the baton with the right hand, and, running on the inside of the lane, passes it to the left hand of the fourth man, who takes it with his left hand just as he enters the straight portion of the track.

Hand to hand contact of right-left pass. Blind.

The inside left pass results in slightly poorer positioning on the second exchange. Also, the danger of dropping the baton while switching the baton to the opposite hand is greater.

The "blind" pass is so named because the outgoing runner makes no attempt to see the baton being placed in his hand. It is his responsibility to begin running at a predetermined moment, place his right or left hand in position to receive the baton, and then accelerate through the passing zone.

The selection of team members will determine when a runner receiving the baton will begin running. Prior to any competition, practice passes will determine the range in which an incoming runner will overtake his teammate. In competition, this range is marked on the track by the outgoing runner somewhere in advance of the passing zone. As the outgoing runner stands at the 10-meter line, he watches his teammate approach the marked spot. As the incoming runner arrives at the spot, the receiver turns and accelerates away from his position as quickly as possible. As he passes over the first zone line, he moves his receiving hand to a position behind his body with his thumb and fingers forming an inverted "V." The incoming runner must place the baton into the "V" with an upward movement (see figure).

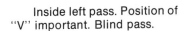

Inside left pass. Position of "V" important. Blind pass.

If the pass is not completed within the pre-planned range, the outgoing runner may slow slightly in the hope of completing the pass before he crosses the last zone line. The outgoing runner must never look to the rear or attempt to reach for the baton. To do so will invariably disrupt the smoothness of the pass and result in a zone violation.

Because of the extreme speed of the sprint relay passes, there is little chance that a poorly timed pass can ever be rectified during a race. Therefore, teammates must be trained to the speed and rhythm of their baton exchange partners. Constant practice will develop the necessary confidence for sprint relay passing.

Sometimes in the 4 × 220, and at all times in longer races, the "sight" or "open" pass is used. If a 4 × 220 team is not experienced, or if they are competing in more than one race where fatigue can affect their timing, the "open" pass is more desirable.

When the open pass is used, the responsibility for completing the pass rests on the outgoing runner. He must time his departure from the first zone line so as to permit the incoming runner to overtake him quickly. The outgoing runner is fresh and well able to judge speed and distance. The incoming runner has the responsibility of holding the baton well ahead of his body where his teammate can grasp the baton and gain speed immediately. As the incoming runner nears the passing zone, his teammate watches his approach. At the proper moment, he begins running, and then reaches to the rear and takes the baton with his right hand. As he turns to run with a full stride, he switches the baton from his right to left hand. Switching the baton immediately reduces the danger of dropping it later when you are tired, or forgetting the switch until you are about to execute the pass.

A well executed "open" pass can improve a team's running potential and reduce its time as much as two or three seconds. If the pass is well executed, each runner will leave the passing zone at a high rate of speed and probably gain on teams who delay or fumble the pass.

CHAPTER 7

THE HURDLES

Hurdling is a sprint race during which the performer is required to clear a fixed number of barriers placed at precise intervals along the running course. The hurdles are constructed of wood and/or metal and consist of two bases with vertical uprights. The two uprights are joined together by one or more cross-bars to form a rectangle frame. The top cross-bar is made of wood with a beveled edge and has a width of 2¾ inches. The surface facing the starting line is white and should have not less than two vertical or diagonal black stripes. The hurdle may be adjustable in height, but must be constructed so that it becomes a fixed and rigid unit at each height to which it is adjusted.

Since starting blocks are used in hurdle races, you should become familiar with their use and function by reading the chapter on sprinting.

In collegiate competition for the 120 high hurdles there are 10 barriers, each 42 inches high; in high school competition the barriers are 39 inches high. The distance from the start line to the first hurdle is 15 yards and from the last hurdle to the finish line is 15 yards. The distance between the hurdles is 10 yards. In the 180 yard high school low hurdles there are eight barriers, 30 inches high, placed 20 yards apart. In the 440 yard college low hurdles there are 10 barriers, each 36 inches high. The distance from the start line to the first hurdle is 45 meters (1 yard = .9144 meter) and the distance from the last hurdle to the finish line is 40 meters. The distance between the hurdles is 35 meters. The use of metric measurement is most efficient in the latter because it avoids the need for calculating fractional parts of a yard in the placement of hurdles.

Each of the three races requires a different technique and training process. The low hurdles require the least technical skill. The intermediate hurdles require the greatest physical strength; the high hurdles require the most technical skill.

THE LOW HURDLES

The start

The start of the low hurdle race is similar to the sprint start; however, as you approach the first hurdle, you must arrive with your feet in position for an uninterrupted hurdle clearance. With this in mind, minor adjustment in the placement of your blocks may be required. It might be necessary to adjust the spacing between the starting blocks, or possibly you will be required to switch the placement of your front and rear foot. Exact block placement is the result of trial and correction. Usually, low hurdlers will take 10 steps to the first hurdle. The feet are placed in the starting blocks with the foot that will lead over the first, and all succeeding hurdles at the rear. In many cases, beginning hurdlers have trouble reaching the first hurdle in 10 steps. If you have this problem, switch your feet and add an extra step. As your starting and sprinting skills improve, you will find that you can reduce the number of steps to 10.

First hurdle clearance

The tall runner has certain advantages in running the low hurdles. First, his center of gravity is usually higher than the hurdle, enabling him to take off closer to the hurdle and land closer to the hurdle after having cleared it. Second, his added height permits a more natural running stride during hurdle clearance, resulting in an efficient unbroken rhythm from start to finish.

The shorter hurdler is required to raise his center of gravity in order to clear the hurdle. Naturally, this results in a loss of running time and can only be compensated for by improving technical skills.

Usually, the low hurdle take-off will be executed 7 feet or more in advance of the hurdle. The exact distance must be determined through repeated practice runs. In clearing the low hurdle it is important to maintain the most natural running form possible. To break this form will usually result in longer flight over the hurdle and delayed landing on the side closer to the finish line.

First hurdle clearance is important in establishing a smooth running rhythm that will aid in maintaining good balance over the other hurdles. Beyond the first hurdle it is important to remain "on stride" in relation to the hurdles. That is, you must learn to be in proper position for the take-off in front of each hurdle.

You can best learn to hurdle by placing a stick on the ground and running over it with a natural stride. As you approach the stick, lift your lead knee in a normal running action. Permit your rear foot to follow in a natural position. Next, raise the stick 4 to 6 inches and repeat the action. Bear in mind that low hurdling is little more than taking a long stride over the barrier. Continue to raise the stick but always maintain the action that approximates a long running stride.

As your practice barrier begins to approximate the height of the low hurdle, you will find it necessary to clear the trail knee. You can best accomplish this by lifting your trail knee out to the side and ro-

Hurdler running over low-positioned stick.

tating your foot to a position parallel to the barrier as shown below. As your foot clears the barrier, continue to bring your knee forward until it reaches a normal running position. Now, drop your foot quickly to the track in front of you. Continue your running action and return to repeat the process.

Beginning hurdlers usually find it difficult to maintain balance from take-off to landing. Generally, loss of balance is the result of improper arm action. During the act of hurdling it is important that the arms and legs synchronize in movement to prevent the body from rotating. The tendency to overwork the arms produces poor foot placement on landing. As your lead leg approaches the hurdle during the take-off, lean toward the hurdle. At the same moment, extend the arm opposite your lead leg forward. The movement of the arm opposite your trail leg should be as close to a normal running action as possible. Above all, it is important that you do not extend this arm to the side. As your lead leg comes down toward the ground, the recovery of your trail leg takes place. When your lead foot strikes the ground, a quick uppercut action of the arm will assist in regaining running speed.

Low hurdle clearance.

Running between hurdles

Between low hurdles it is important to regain running speed as quickly as possible. As you gain experience, you will find that there is little transition from hurdling to sprinting. Immediately after clearing one hurdle your eyes should sight on the top of the next hurdle.

If you lead with your left leg, it is best to run slightly to the left side of your lane. This running position in the lane will permit your lead leg to clear the hurdle and your trail leg to pass completely over the hurdle rather than around the side or beyond the edge. Failure to execute this action properly could result in a disqualification.

The finish

The finish of the low hurdles is similar to the finish of the sprint. It is especially important that you avoid attempting to complete the action of the last hurdle too quickly. If you fail to maintain balance as you leave the last hurdle, you will lose speed at a very critical time in the race. Regain your balance, then drive for the finish line.

THE INTERMEDIATE HURDLES

The intermediate hurdles are a strength event. For the most effective results, the performer is required to run a middle distance event over barriers while maintaining an exact stride pattern from the start to finish. Intermediate hurdling requires moderate hurdling skill for a tall man and excellent skill for a short man. Rhythm is most important in maintaining the continued stride pattern in this event. Once you have attained your running speed, it must be maintained for the duration of the race. A break in stride pattern will result in improper hurdle clearance.

The start

The start of this race is like most other sprint or hurdle races. However, you must arrive at the first hurdle "on stride" if you are to execute an uninterrupted hurdle clearance. During your training, you must establish this pattern with absolute certainty.

For the beginning hurdler, being on stride is more important than being ahead of the other runners at the first hurdle. To this end you should establish a mark on the track about four strides from your first hurdle that can be used to judge your approach to the hurdle. After you sprint out of the blocks, you should begin watching for the mark. If a minor adjustment in your stride is required, make it at this point by hitting the mark exactly. You will now clear the first hurdle in good rhythm and form and probably continue on in the same manner. If your stride adjustment comes at the hurdle, you are most apt to lose time and speed regaining your running stride beyond the hurdle.

In your early training and competition on the intermediate hurdles, you should concentrate on running rhythm between the hurdles. By the time you are ready for competition you should feel you are "flowing between hurdles."

First hurdle clearance

Most hurdlers use between 21 and 23 strides to the first hurdle. You should attempt to cover the distance within this range. Give 22 strides a try. Place your starting blocks on the track with your lead foot in the rear block. Before you start, have a partner stand at your mark about four strides from the first hurdle. He can observe your foot placement and you can judge the control with which you execute the hurdle. Run out of the starting blocks and clear the first hurdle. If your foot placement was good and you cleared the hurdle properly in 22 strides, this number of strides will probably serve you well. However, if you were too close to the hurdle, you may find it necessary to adjust to 21 strides. If you were too far away, you will probably need to adjust to 23 strides. In both instances, you will have to place your lead foot in the front block at the start in order to arrive at the hurdle on an odd number of strides. When you have established your stride pattern to the first hurdle, measure and mark that point for future reference. Thereafter, when practicing, be sure that as you approach the first hurdle, you strive to reach that point accurately with your take-off foot.

Running between hurdles

When you have cleared the first hurdle, continuation to the next must be exact. You should attempt to cover the distance with 15 strides. This stride count means that you will always lead with the same foot. During practice a series of check marks four strides from the hurdle will help you develop a sense of stride and rhythm. When you first begin running the intermediates, learn to run over six or seven hurdles with confidence.

The finish

Even the best-conditioned hurdlers find that the last hurdle is critical and must be approached with extreme care. Naturally, you will be tired and there will be some tendency to become careless. Attempt to maintain your natural running tempo and strive for a perfect take-off position. Speed lost at this point in the race is very difficult to regain because of the energy and power already expended.

The left foot lead

It is generally best to learn to run the intermediate hurdles with your left foot leading over the hurdles. Since the race is run around an oval track, landing with your left foot will permit you to lean to the inside and maintain a smooth circular course. It also permits you to run closer to the inside of your lane, thereby reducing the distance you will run during the total race. If you lead with your right foot, you will be forced to approach each hurdle from an exact right angle, producing a flattening of the turn at each hurdle. This flattened course will result in your having to run a slightly greater distance between each hurdle, and it will require a slight cross-over step immediately after clearing each hurdle.

Left foot lead over low hurdle.

Lead foot switching

Some hurdlers who are unable to execute the distance between hurdles with 15 strides switch the lead foot and use 16 strides. In this case, they clear the first hurdle with their left foot, the second with their right foot, the third with their left foot, and so on to the end. While not the most efficient method, this pattern of hurdling enables the man with a short stride to participate with a reasonable degree of success.

Other hurdlers use lead foot switching to adjust to fatigue or track conditions. If they must run a given part of their race into a strong wind, they may shorten their stride and switch their lead leg to conserve energy. If during the running of the last two or three hurdles, fatigue prevents proper stride length, they will switch. Needless to say, there is a price to be paid for the switching action: the distance of one stride for each time the switch is used. Good hurdlers will use the technique sparingly and only when experience indicates that it is necessary for the completion of the race.

You obviously have advantages if you are capable of leading over the hurdles with either foot, so practice the technique, but use it only at the proper moment.

THE HIGH HURDLES

The high hurdles require an exact skill from beginning to end. The technique of running this event can be developed only through constant re-evaluation during practice and constant adjustment and correction during the competitive race. Although this fact is true in all hurdle races, the degree of attention and control must be greatest in the high hurdles.

The start

The start of the high hurdle race is probably more critical than any other. Not only will you be required to move at the highest possible controlled speed, but you must also arrive at the first hurdle exactly on stride for the take-off.

The placement of your starting blocks will depend on whether you use seven, eight, or nine strides to the first hurdle. If you use seven or nine strides, your lead foot will be to the rear in the starting blocks. If you use eight strides, your lead foot will be forward. Selection of your stride pattern will depend on your ability to accelerate out of the starting blocks, the length of your stride, and your take-off distance in front of the hurdle.

Generally, the execution of the start is similar to the sprint start, except that hurdlers tend to become more erect in their running position before they arrive at the first hurdle. The more erect position results in a slightly higher hip carriage, thereby reducing the distance the hips must be lifted for hurdle clearance. Long before you attempt your first start and hurdle clearance, you must learn the techniques of hurdling.

Hurdle clearance

It is advisable to learn high hurdle technique "from the ground up," as in the low hurdle event. The procedures used in learning the low hurdles should be studied and mastered. However, since the extreme height of the hurdles must be considered, more exacting techniques must be learned. While the action of the lead leg is similar to that used in the low hurdles, because of the added height of the barrier, the upper leg must be lifted higher and the lower leg must not extend until it has reached the height of the hurdle.

The action of the trail leg is quite different from that in the low hurdles. In the high hurdle event, your trail leg and foot must be flattened out as they pass over the hurdle. This movement requires a high degree of flexibility that must be developed while learning to run the high hurdles. Because you will be forced to raise your center of gravity higher in this event, there is a natural delay in action before you return to the ground. During this delay, you must maintain exact balance and move to an efficient running position before your foot strikes the ground on the side of the hurdle closer to the finish line.

In learning the high hurdle clearance it is best to use a breakaway plastic top on the hurdle, or a light barrier that will not produce severe knee or leg injury.

Depending on the various factors related to your stride pattern and block placement at the start, somewhere between 6½ and 7½ feet in front of the hurdle you will execute the take-off. As your center of gravity, located near your hips, begins to rise, your upper body will begin to move forward and downward. This action is accomplished through the movement of your lead arm and the relaxing of your lower back muscles. As your lead foot drives up over the hurdle, your opposite arm will extend forward to a position level with and alongside your lead foot. You are now leaning toward the ground on the far side of the hurdle. As your trail foot leaves the ground, it must rotate outward with the knee. Your trail knee will come to a position where it is momentarily tucked slightly forward of your armpit. As your lead leg passes over the hurdle it begins to drop toward the ground, and it strikes the ground moving backward so as to help maintain your forward speed. Meanwhile, your trail knee has been carried forward in a high knee running position. If you do not attempt to hurry this movement, your center of gravity will pass over your lead foot just as it strikes the ground and you will lose a minimum of running speed. As you clear the hurdle, your eyes should focus on the next hurdle. Once you contact the ground, you are a sprinter moving to the next hurdle.

The action of your arms during high hurdling is critical. They must help you maintain balance. To this end, you must control the position of both arms exactly. Remember that your legs are doing the running and your arms must synchronize with them. In effect, as either of your legs moves upward, the opposite arm must move downward to maintain balance. Conversely, as either leg moves downward, the opposite arm must move upward. Naturally, when your trail knee and foot rotate outward, your opposite arm must move outward for balance. It then becomes important to bring your trail leg through as close to your body as possible. This will permit your opposite arm to remain close to your body and provide good running action as you return to the ground. The sign of a master technician of the hurdles is his arm action over and between the hurdles.

Running between hurdles

The 10 yards between hurdles is used to regain running speed. During clearance of the hurdle, speed is lost because you are not in contact with the ground for a relatively extended period. When you return to the ground, you must begin running again. High, fast knee action will help you regain top running speed and also maintain your center of gravity at the highest possible running position. Maintaining this high center of gravity position makes it possible for you to clear the next hurdle with a minimum of rise, a factor important to maintaining speed between the hurdles.

The finish

When you clear the last hurdle, 15 yards of running remains. However, there is no longer need to maintain a perfect stride pattern. Increase the power stroke of your arms and drive hard toward the finish with your legs. Continue your sprinting action to a point 10 yards beyond the finish, and you will often overtake the runner who feels the race has ended at the last hurdle.

PRACTICE SESSIONS

Hurdle practice sessions will naturally be based on the particular event in which you plan to participate. The high hurdles will demand the most technical practice and the low hurdles the least. However, it will be important that you prepare for your effort with a proper warm-up period and a definite period of skill practice. The warm-up for hurdle practice is often longer than for other track events because of the extreme degrees of flexion that are demanded of the body.

During early season practice you are better off running and hurdling on the grass. There is less danger of injury to the legs and torso in the event of a spill, and the soft surface will help strengthen your legs because it will require slightly more effort to execute the strong lift off the ground.

When your body is conditioned and your legs are prepared for hard work, divide your practice sessions into units that will progress through to the final technique.

Unit one should be concerned with developing the most natural running action possible over the hurdles. Place a stick on the ground and run back and forth across it. When you can execute this move without any change in running technique, raise the stick a few inches and repeat the crossing drill. As you near the stick, do not extend your leg to execute the crossing, but lift your knee and run over it. Continue to move the stick upward while maintaining natural form. If you begin to experience difficulty with loss of balance, reduce the action of your arms. Bend your elbows and hook your thumbs in the arm holes of your shirt. In this way your arm carriage will be very close to your body. With repeated practice you will find that you can

CORRECTION CHART

Error	Causes	Corrections
1. Unable to reach first hurdle on stride.	a. Improper block placement.	a. Switch positions of front and rear blocks.
		b. Adjust blocks to permit longer first stride.
2. Excessively high clearance.	a. Take-off point too close to hurdle.	a. Move take-off point farther from hurdle.
3. Hitting trail knee on hurdle.	a. Upper body too erect during clearance.	a. Relax lower back muscles and dive into hurdle with chest close to lead knee.
	b. Trail knee not drawn up to knee-chest position after take-off.	b. Draw knee quickly forward after take-off.
4. Loss of balance over hurdle.	a. Excessive movement of arm across body.	a. Maintain arm movement across body to within position of lead leg.
	b. Wide swing of trail leg.	b. Maintain swing of lower part of trail leg within extreme limit of trail knee.
	c. Shoulder rotation during take-off.	c. Maintain shoulders at right angles to track at all times.
	d. Too much sweeping action of arm on lead leg side during clearance.	d. Keep arm on lead leg side flexed and close to body.
5. Loss of speed after clearing hurdle.	a. Loss of balance over hurdle.	a. See all of above.
	b. Lead foot touching ground in advance of center of gravity.	b. Sweep lead foot down and back toward track as you reach for the ground with your toe.
	c. Trail foot returning to track too quickly.	c. Bring trail knee forward after clearing hurdle.
	d. Incomplete arm action upon landing.	d. When your lead foot returns to track, begin hard arm action. Swing elbows forcefully.

execute an efficient hurdle clearance with little or no outward action of your arms. Your legs will be doing the greater part of the work. Next, free your thumbs, but maintain good arm position. As the stick is moving upward, you will come to a point where your trail foot is beginning to hit the stick. You are ready for unit two when this occurs.

Unit two should be used to develop outward rotation of the trail foot. This can be developed by working over the side of the hurdle. Place the hurdles in normal position. On the side closer to the start line make a scratch mark on the ground about 6 or 7 feet from the hurdle. The distance will depend on your ability to gain speed and execute the proper moves. On the side closer to the finish line place another mark about 3 or 4 feet from the hurdle. Run alongside the hurdles. As your trail foot hits the first mark, pass your lead foot alongside the hurdle concentrating on having it contact the ground at the second scratch mark. Lift your trail foot upward and to the outside so as to pass over the hurdle in a flattened position. Bring your knee forward into the running position and continue on to the next hurdle. Repeat this action over as many hurdles as possible. As you improve this technique, you will be able to concentrate on improved arm action.

Hurdler over side of low hurdle.

Start with a low hurdle and move the hurdle higher only when you have established a smooth running action over the present height. The number of steps used between hurdles during this form of practice is not particularly important. Developing the proper leg action is the goal of your routine.

In your third unit you should hurdle over the barrier and begin to develop normal striding followed by good trail leg action. Locate the hurdles in their normal position. From a standing start position, run through a few approaches until you have established a take-off spot. Now hurdle with the best possible form. The action of your trail leg will be critical during this form of training. You must carry your knee high as you leave the hurdle. Unless you attain a full stride coming off the hurdle, you will be unable to reach the next hurdle at the proper take-off position.

During your fourth unit, introduce the starting blocks and develop the ability to move off the blocks and into your stride pattern quickly. As you leave the starting blocks, concentrate on high knee action and powerful arm coordination. As a beginning hurdler, allow for a little extra clearance over the first hurdle. Approach the hurdle at the fastest possible controlled speed. Do not sprint blindly at the hurdle. Getting to the hurdle first is of no value if you cannot execute a smooth, rhythmic take-off.

When you become reasonably skilled, you can place hurdles at irregular distances and develop a sense of timing and judgment that will help you adjust your stride pattern. If in the course of hurdling you should hit one of the barriers, the ability to make an immediate correction will improve your stride. This form of practice can add a measure of fun to your learning and sharpen your ability as a hurdler.

COUNTDOWN

Prior to running a flight of hurdles, you should quickly review how you may best accomplish the effort by asking these questions.

1. Are my starting blocks properly set?
2. As I run out of the starting blocks, on what fact must I concentrate?
3. How will high knee action help my hurdle approach?
4. What part will arm and leg coordination play in my hurdling?
5. During hurdle clearance, what must I attempt to accomplish?
6. Should I be concerned with the position of other runners during the progress of the race?

SAFETY PRECAUTIONS

Whenever possible, practice on grass surfaces during the early season so as to protect yourself in the event of a fall. Never run over hurdles that are not properly located in the knockdown position and be sure that there are no ruts or stones in your lane.

When they are available, practice over hurdles with plastic breakaway tops. When you become fatigued, switch to a different activity, such as cross-country running or jogging. The danger of serious injury increases when your body is tired.

In the event of an injury or abrasion, seek immediate medical treatment.

CHAPTER 8

CROSS-COUNTRY

Cross-country running is probably one of the most enjoyable forms of running you will experience. Removed from the track, it provides an opportunity to compete over natural land contours, through woods, fields, and meadows.

As a training ground for runners who will compete in other events, it offers a chance to run at varied distances and paces without the constant presence of the stop watch. The continued change of scenery seems to provide the average runner with mental refreshment. Ten miles on the track seems endless, but 10 miles through the woods seems to pass in a minimum of time.

While the short, light-framed man seems to be more common among cross country runners, there seems to be no ideal body type. Tall men have performed well, and medium-build, rugged men have faired equally well.

Training for cross-country is usually divided into two forms: quality and quantity.

Quality work is related to speed and cardiovascular development. There is evidence to indicate that repeatedly increasing the pulse rate rapidly and following with short periods of rest will increase cardiovascular efficiency. Training over distances of 220 yards, 330 yards, and sometimes 440 yards provides an opportunity to increase your pulse rate to a high tempo. During an easy jog following a fast run, your pulse will begin to return to normal. Before it returns to normal, you again repeat your fast run. If you can regulate your runs so that they occur each time your pulse rate reaches 130 beats, you will probably find that you are able to repeat the runs, and at the same time you will be assisting strong cardiovascular development.

Wearing an ordinary wrist watch with a sweep second hand can facilitate pulse count. When you have completed a run, record your pulse for 10 seconds and multiply the count by six. When your pulse beat reaches 23 or 22 for 10 seconds, you are ready to run again.

Although many people find it difficult to locate their own pulse at a normal rate, a pulse of 130 beats can usually be found at the wrist with little difficulty. In fact, with some training you can learn to detect your pulse by watching your wrist when the count is high.

Speed running slightly below your maximum ability will also help to develop the ability to run faster for longer periods. As you train your muscles to relax under the demand of speed, you run more efficiently. Therefore, you can continue for longer periods before fatigue begins to take its heavy toll on your system.

It is difficult to say how fast you should run in speed runs. However, if you can run at a pace you consider about three-quarters of your maximum effort, you will be engaged in effective speed work.

Quality work can also take the form of longer runs, but never equal to the distance of your race. Repeated runs of 880 yards, or three-quarters of a mile, can be classed as quality. In each case these distances should be run faster than race pace, and the run repeated when your body is close to rested from the last effort.

Quantity work concerns itself with long distance running. During the quantity workout you will be running distances greater than your course. Usually, a distance double your course length will provide a good quantity workout. However, many variations of distance are possible.

STRIDE

Unlike the track stride, a cross-country stride is variable and must be changed to accommodate the changing land contours. When you are running on flat country, your stride should be rolling in nature. As your foot touches the ground, you should attempt to land on the rear portion, roll forward to the ball of your foot, and lift off with a minimum of leg extension. Running "on your toes" can cause considerable leg fatigue long before you have neared the finish line.

When running uphill, you must be careful not to overstride. Reaching too far forward will produce a shock effect on your legs and hamper your stride. During uphill runs you must concentrate on normal arm lift position, but you must attempt to increase the force of your arm movements. If the hill is short, attack it: gain a little extra momentum before you reach the hill, and clear the top without slowing. If the hill is long, run into it at a normal pace and attempt to maintain your pace. Work harder as you move higher. At the top of the hill, accelerate; you must not rest. In a close race, victory belongs to the man who runs over the top of a hill.

Downhill running poses another problem completely. If executed improperly, it is very tiring. Once again, your arms become very important. In this case they provide the balance needed to control your stride. Most runners tend to carry their arms slightly wider than when running uphill. This position helps prevent loss of balance if you overstride. When running downhill, attempt to prevent an overstride by not lifting off the ball of your foot. Keep your feet close to the ground. Near the bottom of the hill, let your speed increase, and maintain it for the longest possible distance.

If the terrain is extremely rough, run with short, quick strides. Maintain a more erect position and concentrate on knee lift and body balance. Forget the relative position of your opponents and concern yourself with each step as you make it. Watch out for areas covered with fallen leaves. They can hide stones, branches, or holes, and in the late fall they can be very slippery. You should rarely attempt to pass other runners in rough terrain. Pass immediately before reaching it, or pass immediately after leaving it.

If the terrain is soft, wet, or slippery, shorten your stride so as to improve your balance and reduce the danger of an overstride that can cause you to fall.

If the course contains any obstacles that must be jumped, approach them carefully with a short stride. When possible, study the obstacle before the race so you will know how to cope with it best. Approaching a low fence, shorten your stride and prepare to jump quickly. If the fence top is broad enough for good foot placement, lift your lead foot onto the top and as your weight comes onto that leg, push off quickly. If the fence top is narrow, hurdle it without any contact. In the case of higher barriers, place your hand on the top rail and vault the obstacle.

If you must pass through water, know the bottom surface before you run through it, and know the depth of the water. If the bottom is hard and the water shallow, lengthen your stride and move through it quickly. If the water is deep or the bottom is soft, shorten your stride and lift your knees.

A good cross-country running stride is the result of practice. You will develop a good stride only if you take the time to work at it. Balance and control are the keys to efficient movement. In cross-country running, your balance will change with every change in land contour. Learn how best to accomplish your run over the terrain through constant practice.

CROSS-COUNTRY COURSES

All cross-country courses differ. Above all, you should get to know your own course so well that you have a distinct advantage over any opponent you will meet on your home course.

Through practice runs over different segments of your course, you can come to know how fast you should cover a particular segment, or how difficult it may be to run. On those parts of the course that will provide the greatest challenge to your opponents, know your maximum capability and run hard. Use these areas for overtaking your opponent or increasing your lead. If you find a segment of the course where you run particularly well, use this area to your advantage.

During practice, learn your capacity at different distances and over the total distance. With this knowledge you can often force your opponent to run hard when he does not wish to, or you can cause him to give up the pace for fear of not finishing the race.

There are various theories about the advantages of running at an even pace throughout the race, of starting fast and settling to a slower pace toward the end, and of starting slow and building speed toward the end. Generally, how you run a cross-country course will depend on your condition, your knowledge of the course, and your knowledge of your opponents. However, certain rules of cross-country running cannot be avoided. In a race with many runners, you must stay with the front runners during the early stages of the race. In a race with only a few runners, attempt to stay with your team's best runners for as long as possible. Cross-country races often develop into separate races among small groups of runners. The closer you can keep to the front group in the early stages of the race, the stronger your position will be at the finish of the race. When you pass an opponent in cross-country, pass him with a strong move, and maintain it until you are well ahead of him. Do not let him entertain any thought of ever challenging you again. In a large group of runners, avoid having to weave in and out of the field. Move to the outside edge of the group and run a straight line. Weaving results in a constant change of pace and produces fatigue very quickly.

PRACTICE SESSIONS

Cross-country practice sessions must be planned well in advance of your first competition.

During your pre-season practice, you must work long and hard to develop the strength of your legs and to meet the demands that will be placed on you later.

When your legs and body have toughened to some degree, you must begin a varied program of speed and distance. Usually it is advisable to alternate days of speed with days of distance work. After a high quality workout, your body will usually benefit from a relatively easy quantity workout.

During the competitive season, you will need to increase the quality of your work. There is no such thing as rest during this period. The effect of training is cumulative as your body learns to absorb the punishment of hard training. During the competitive training period, you must remind yourself that each day of hard work will result in an easier race when competition finally arrives. Your training needs during this period will be based on your prime weakness. If you need speed, emphasize it; if you need distance, run, run, run.

During the competition season, you are limited by what you have done during the early training periods. You no longer have time to develop your total running ability. Your program will settle into a pattern of quality work, rest, compete. If you have trained properly and learned the skills well, you will probably enjoy the experience and find yourself well trained for winter competition.

Cross-country running requires a complete training program. The conditioning chapter in this book can serve as a guide to proper strength development and workout plan. The progression of your program must be based on a year-to-year improvement in your total physical condition, so do not attempt to advance too quickly in your first year.

EQUIPMENT

Because of the special nature of cross-country running, a little more consideration than usual must be given to equipment.

Generally, the same uniforms are worn for cross-country and track. However, if you live in colder regions of the United States, some special equipment is advisable.

During cold weather, wear wool hats that can be pulled over your ears and gloves. Thermal underwear or lamb's wool shirts should be worn as a minimum protection. If it is particularly cold, wear long underwear.

Cross-country shoes must be selected on the basis of the course to be run. Some courses are almost entirely hard roads. In this case, a rubber-soled shoe is necessary. However, when the course goes over grass or dirt, you are probably better off with a spiked shoe. The length of your spikes must be carefully selected. In the early fall they can be short, but as the leaves begin to fall you are better off with a slightly longer spike. When you travel to another course, bring all your shoes. Test the course well before the race and decide which of your shoes you want to wear. Never trust the weather or the course. Arrive prepared to run in your best suitable equipment.

SCORING

The scoring of cross-country differs from track and is an important part of your knowledge about the sport.

A cross-country team consists of seven men, unless otherwise agreed. In dual meets a maximum of 12 men may be entered, but only the first seven to finish on each team enter into the scoring.

First place scores 1 point; second place, 2; third place, 3; and so on. All men who finish the course are ranked and tallied in this manner. The team score then is determined by totaling the points scored by the first five men of each team to finish. The team scoring the smallest number of points is the winner. If less than five finish, the places of all members of that team are disregarded. If the total points scored by two or more teams are the same, it is a tie.

MARKINGS

The course should be properly measured and marked by one or more of the following methods, in order of preference:

1. Tall sign posts with large directional arrows on boards, fastened to the tops of the posts so that the arrows will be plainly visible at a distance to contestants approaching the posts. These posts should be placed at every point that the course turns, and should also be placed wherever there is any doubt as to the direction of travel.

2. A lime line laid on the ground along the entire distance of the route to be traveled by the contestants.

3. Flags, as follows: (a) A red flag to indicate a turn to the left; (b) A yellow flag to indicate a turn to the right; and (c) A blue flag to indicate the course is straight ahead. The flags mark the shortest perimeter of the course.

COUNTDOWN

Before you enter a cross-country competition, there are many questions you should be able to answer.

1. Are you familiar with the course and all markings?

2. Does the weather warrant any special considerations?

3. Do you know the exact location of the finish line, and what the procedure will be at the finish?

4. Are you aware of the starting commands and starting signal?

5. What is your plan for the start? How will you adjust if you fail to attain the position you desire?

6. If you have a primary opponent, what is the color of his uniform?

SAFETY PRECAUTIONS

Most of the safety precautions related to cross-country running have been discussed in detail throughout this unit. A few general comments will add to your knowledge.

Running on roads, you should always move against traffic. If you must cross a road, do not depend on the driver of a car to see you. He will least expect to see a runner during late evening hours, so if you run at this time, wear some form of reflective clothing.

Take particular care of your feet. In warm weather, rub a light coating of soap on your feet to reduce friction between your skin and your shoe. During practice, if you suspect you are getting a blister, stop and put something on it or remove the cause immediately. Have any injury treated by competent medical personnel.

CHAPTER 9

THE DISCUS

The discus throw requires speed, strength, and agility. It is among the most graceful events of track and field. It is not uncommon for apparently stronger men to be outdistanced in the throw by men who have developed the grace and technique needed to master the event.

The discus is circular, made of wood or plastic with a smooth metal rim. Metal plates are set flush into the side of the body of the discus at its exact center to give the discus the correct weight. The high school discus weighs 3 lb. 9 oz.; the college discus is 4 lb. 6.4 oz.

The discus is thrown from a circle 98½ inches in diameter. It is usually constructed of cement or some other all-weather material. The circle should be divided into a front and rear half by lines outside of and on each side of the circle. The landing area, called the sector, is marked by two radial lines passing through the exact center of the circle and forming an interior angle of 60°.

THE GRIP

The discus grip requires that the discus be suspended on the last joint of the four fingers while the thumb is placed flat along the side. The palm is held slightly away from the surface, resulting in a talon-like grip, resembling that of a bird.

From this point on, the directions are for a right-handed discus thrower.

Discus lying in hand. Notice finger positions.

You should begin learning to roll the discus before attempting to throw it. Hold your right hand palm upward, level with your hip. Spread your fingers in a relaxed position. Lay the discus on your right hand so the first joints of your fingers curl slightly around the edge. Your thumb should be out of sight and supporting the discus. Lower your hand to your right side and permit the discus to hang on your fingers. The discus should now be between your right leg and your hand, with your palm facing your leg. Position your hand so that your index finger and second finger support the greater part of the weight of the discus. In this position, the lowest point of the discus will be located between these two fingers.

Discus in ready-to-roll position.

Now, bend your knee so as to bring your hand almost to the ground. Swing the discus to the rear and then forward. As the discus passes the lowest point in the forward swing, roll it out of your hand with a clockwise rotation. If you execute this movement properly, the discus will roll along its vertical axis until it loses momentum.

This action should be repeated until you can produce the desired results with regularity. To make your practice an interesting challenge in accuracy, roll the discus back and forth with a partner to see whose discus travels in the straighter line.

Rolling discus away from body.

When you have mastered this skill, it is time to learn the technique of "dragging the discus." Hold the discus in the proper grip and permit it to hang at your side. Locate a straight line, or mark a straight line on the ground. Now, begin walking in a tight circle while progressing along the line. If you allow your throwing arm to hang completely loosely, it will begin to fall to the rear of your hip as your turning action "drags" it around the circle. As your momentum increases, the discus will begin to rise toward a position parallel to the surface of the ground. If you suddenly step out of the circular rotation by taking a wide step with your left foot, the discus will tend to swing out and away from your body. As it does, force your right hip and then your right shoulder ahead of the discus and "sling" it away from your body with the same type of movement you used to roll it out of your hand. Repeat this sequence of actions until you have developed the desirable drag. Remember, the discus must always travel in a position to the rear of your hip as you travel in the tight circle. Do not attempt to bring your arm to a position parallel to the ground by lifting it yourself; the lifting action results from the rotational force of your body turning inside the wider course of the discus.

You are now ready to move into the discus circle.

LEAD-UP SKILLS

For purposes of clarity, consider the discus circle to be marked like the face of a clock. As you stand to the rear of the circle looking toward the landing sector, a line drawn through the apex and bisecting the landing sector represents 12 o'clock. On the right is 3 o'clock, at the rear of the circle is 6 o'clock, and on the left is 9 o'clock.

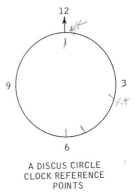

Diagram of discus circle with clock face plan.

A DISCUS CIRCLE
CLOCK REFERENCE
POINTS

Stand at the center of the circle with your right foot pointed toward 4 o'clock. Place your left foot toward 12 o'clock about 24 inches from your right. Point your left toe toward 2 o'clock and align it with your right heel. Flex your right knee so that your weight is now primarily supported on the ball of your right foot. Rotate your head and shoulders until your chest is pointed toward 6 o'clock. Raise your left arm with the elbow bent to a position level with your shoulders. Your elbow should point toward 6 o'clock and your forearm should be at right angles to your upper arm. Permit the discus to hang at your side in the proper grip position.

While maintaining your weight on your right foot, swing your right hip and hand gently toward 3 o'clock. Without stopping, reverse your swing so as to come back through 6 o'clock and around to 11 o'clock with your right hip and right arm. During the back swing, permit your right arm to swing slightly away from your body. Now, reverse your direction again by pushing with the ball of your right foot and rotating forward onto your left foot. The rapid shift of your weight will produce a position wherein the arm holding the discus will fall behind your hip as the rotation begins. As your chest and shoulders turn forward ahead of the discus, let the discus drag behind you. As it comes around, it will tend to swing out and away from your body. Let it swing until your right shoulder reaches 3 o'clock and your left shoulder is at 9 o'clock. At this point, "sling" the discus farther out and away by exaggerating the pull of your right shoulder.

Discus thrower in position at center of circle.

Release position. Palm facing ground and wrist slightly cocked.

It is important during the rotational movement to keep your head and shoulders directly over your hips. This position will help maintain the discus in the drag position and permit a more effective release as the discus reaches the 3 o'clock position. Remember that the release of the discus takes place off your index finger and the discus must rotate through the air with a clockwise rotation.

Practice the beginning throw until you feel you can execute the move with gentle control. Then, increase the speed of your movements. The more you increase speed, the more the discus will tend to pull away from your body during rotation. The amount of resistance your body produces to the pull-away force of the discus will govern the distance the discus will travel after its release.

At the moment of release, your palm should be facing toward the ground and your arm should be extended at shoulder level. The rim of the discus, or blade, as it is sometimes called, should be inclined about 25° above a line parallel with the ground. This position of the discus is called the angle of inclination or tilt. It should not be confused with the angle of projection, or flight path, which refers to the relative angle at which the center of gravity of the discus travels away from parallel to the ground.

ADVANCED TECHNIQUES

There are two generally accepted methods of throwing the discus: the old style, the one and one-half turn, and the newer style, the one and three-quarters turn. There exist some good arguments for learning the former at the beginning of your training: (1) The technique requires that you be in contact with the ground for a longer period. Contact with the ground helps reduce the chances of critical errors. (2) This turn develops somewhat less explosively and so produces a more flowing, controlled action. (3) There is less tendency to move the discus out of the drag position in this turn.

The One and One-Half Turn

The one and one-half turn starts at the rear of the circle, using the same orientation with the clock face that you used during the beginning throw. Stand in the circle with your right foot at 6 o'clock and your left foot spread about 15 inches toward 12 o'clock. Both feet should be pointed at right angles to the base reference line running from 6 o'clock to 12 o'clock. Your shoulders should be in a normal position, and the discus should be hanging at your side.

Bring your left arm with the elbow bent to shoulder level with your forearm parallel to your shoulders. Rotate your body forward so that your weight shifts to your left foot and the discus swings over your left foot. Reverse, so that your weight now swings back onto your right foot as your knee flexes slightly. Your body should continue to rotate to the rear, until your chest is pointed toward 6 o'clock and your right arm has moved to a position at right angles to the base reference line and slightly away from and to the rear of your hip. The ball of your left foot remains in contact with the ground.

The spin

Action is initiated by a pivoting push with your right foot. At the same time, your left foot pivots and receives the weight of your body. As you pivot, the left knee must flex slightly. During the pivot, the left knee leads the movement and your chest and hip follow slightly behind your knee. Your right arm must be permitted to relax and to be dragged along by your upper body. Your left toe continues to pivot until it is pointed at 10 o'clock on the circle. At this point your right foot, which has also been pivoting, leaves the surface of the circle, and steps to a position at the center of the circle with the toe pointed toward 10 o'clock and the knee flexed. Your right foot now pivots at the center of the circle while your body turns and permits your left foot to move up the base reference line to a position slightly to the left of 12 o'clock, with your toe pointed toward 1 o'clock.

During this pivoting movement, it is important that your hips and shoulders remain behind your lead knee, and that your arm and discus drag behind your right hip. When your pivoting right foot reaches a position where your toe is pointed toward 4 o'clock on the circle, the ball of your right foot is driven hard into the ground, and your right hip and shoulder are brought vigorously forward to produce maximum pull against the discus. At this moment your left foot must be in solid contact with the surface of the circle. Your left knee is slightly flexed. As your shoulders and hips come around the circle to a position at right angles to the base reference line, your right arm is pulled forcefully into the throw and the discus is released when it reaches shoulder level and is as far away from your body as possible. At the same moment, your left leg is extended to add slightly more lift to the throw.

The reverse

After the discus is released, your body is still moving in a rapid circular direction. You will tend to leave the ground immediately following the release. When you do, pull your left leg to the rear and reach for the ground with your right foot. Land on the ball of your right foot and continue to spin until your rotation has slowed enough to permit you to regain balance on both feet. Now, walk out the back half of the circle.

If you think back, you will realize that the beginning throw was the final stage of your complete one and one-half turn. You have added the spin to attain greater speed. Failure to treat the spin as more than a controlled entry into the beginning throw will usually produce wild, uncontrolled throws.

A one and one-half turn throw is sufficient to produce fine results with firm control over your movements. If you are able to master

this technique, you may wish to try the most modern technique—
the one and three-quarter turn.

The One and Three-Quarters Turn

Using the same clock reference as before, face the rear of the
circle and place your right foot at 6 o'clock with your toe directed
slightly toward the left. Your left foot is placed laterally, about 8 inches
from your right. Hang the discus at your side, and bring your left arm
to shoulder level position. Flex both knees, and assume a semi-squat
position. Swing the discus forward toward your left foot. As you do so,
move your left foot to the base line of reference so that it is pointing
at nearly right angles to the line. Next, swing the discus to the rear,
lifting it away from your body as it goes back. Your shoulders and hips
must move to the rear until your left shoulder points toward 6 o'clock
and your right arm is carried as far toward 12 o'clock as possible. In
this position, you are "wound up tight" with the discus well behind
your right hip and shoulder.

Starting position for one and three-
quarters turn.

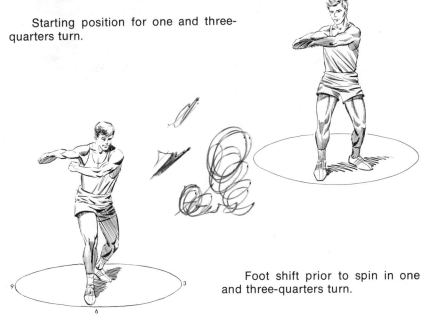

Foot shift prior to spin in one
and three-quarters turn.

The spin

Movement begins as you forcefully rotate the ball of your right
foot toward 12 o'clock. As your weight shifts onto your pivoting left
foot, your right knee is driven around the circle, with your right thigh
in a position parallel to the ground. This movement and position
produce a circular hop, during which both feet are off the ground

CORRECTION CHART

Error	Causes	Corrections
1. Low delivery.	a. Discus moving ahead of hip.	a. Hold left arm as far to the rear as possible during spin.
	b. No extension of left leg prior to delivery.	b. Try to land at front of circle with left leg in flexed position.
	c. No inclination of hand during release.	c. Incline your thumb about 25 degrees above parallel with the ground during final pull through.
2. High delivery.	a. Too much weight on rear foot at moment of delivery.	a. Drive your foot hard against the ground to initiate delivery motion. Transfer your weight forward to your left foot.
	b. Lifting the arm independently of the hip, or ahead of the hip.	b. Allow your angle of delivery to be established by the movement and angle of your hip when delivering the throw. Do not lift your arm or hand upward.
	c. Forcing the discus downward as your right foot lands at the center of the circle.	c. Drag the discus through the turn. Do not attempt to establish a delivery angle by hand or arm movement.

while your body rotates in a semi-squat. It might be helpful to think of this turn as a sprinting rotation during which your back leads the movement and your body moves as far ahead of the discus as possible. As your body rotates through the air, you must wait until your feet arrive in the position from which you deliver the beginning throw.

During the spin action of the one and three-quarters turn, you must concentrate on maintaining perfect balance. Your body must first wind as a spring into a tight coiled position. Your thigh must travel parallel to the ground and remain in that position until your right foot returns to the ground with your knee in a flexed position. At the instant that your right foot returns to the ground, your left foot must be driving for the ground, slightly to the left of the base line of reference, with your toe pointed toward 2 o'clock and your knee flexed. When both feet return to the ground, you must execute a powerful pull from your right foot. The discus, now travelling low at 7 o'clock, is pulled with tremendous force into the release. The release and reverse occur just as in the one and one-half turn.

CORRECTION CHART *(Continued)*

Error	Causes	Corrections
3. Discus landing to right of sector.	a. Improper landing position of right foot at the center of the circle.	a. Check for desired foot placement at completion of the spin.
	b. Left foot landing to right side of base reference line.	b. Increase power of spin so as to get completely around turn. Delay drop of left foot to surface of circle.
	c. Early extension of right leg after landing at center of circle.	c. Delay extension of right foot until left foot touches near base reference line.
4. Incorrect rotation of discus.	a. Improper grip or hand position at moment of delivery.	a. Release discus off index finger.
		b. Keep thumb pointed in desired direction of throw.
5. Discus wobbles during flight.	a. Too much finger contact with blade.	a. Permit only the first joints of fingers to enclose the blade.
	b. Palm of hand in contact with surface of discus.	b. Maintain talon grip with palm not in contact with center of discus.

PRACTICE SESSIONS

The organization of a practice session is extremely important. It should retain some carry-over from the session before and progress into new areas when your skills indicate you are ready. One session may only be sufficient to move you part way through a given unit. Most important, each session or unit must have a specific goal.

Although you may quickly learn to roll the discus along the ground, the skill of throwing will take long periods of practice. Your first practice unit should concern itself with learning to deliver the discus efficiently. Your grip will become very important.

Stand at the center of the circle in proper throwing position. Permit the discus to hang between your palm and the side of your right leg. Flex your right knee and swing the discus toward 9 o'clock. Your left arm, shoulders, and hips must be in proper position. Now, reverse the direction of swing and rotate your knee, foot, and right hip in the direction of 3 o'clock. As the discus passes through the low point of the swing, at about 6 o'clock, extend your knee forcefully and continue rotation. The discus will press hard against your fingers as it tries to pull out of your hand. Thrust your chest into a high angle and pull the discus into a high angle of release. Throw it nearly vertically. Your purpose here is to learn the feeling of the discus pulling hard against your fingers as your legs pull the other way.

If your fingers have not learned to control the weight of the discus, it will slip away from you as you pull against it. Throwing the discus at a steep angle usually permits you to exercise a little more control over the angle of the blade. It will tend not to wobble excessively.

As you master control of the blade angle, lower the angle of your delivery and attempt to maintain the angle of the blade on a consistent plane. Above all, be sure the discus is maintained in the drag position throughout this unit.

In your second unit, work to establish good rotational thrust into the delivery. You are concerned here with the transfer of your weight to the left foot. Stand in proper position for a standing throw. Swing the discus around toward 9 o'clock and permit your left foot to lift slightly off the surface of the circle. As the discus reaches 9 o'clock, drop your left toe to the circle. This action will produce a slight weight shift forward and a rotational movement toward 3 o'clock. Now, extend your knee and rotate your foot to drive your right hip and shoulder ahead of the discus. As the discus comes past 6 o'clock, transfer your weight to the ball of your left foot and extend your knee. At this moment your arm should be parallel to the ground and as far from your body as possible.

Care must be taken during this unit to wait for the left foot to establish the minor rotation and lift as it strikes the ground. Any force exerted against the discus prior to this moment will cause the body to be pulled to the rear of the circle, and the throw will be executed improperly off the right leg.

Remember that you are attempting to establish rotation around the left hip, leg, and foot. Your left side must "block" or hold against the right side rotation. In this way it establishes a pivot point around which the right side of the body rotates.

Your third unit can concern itself with moving from the rear to the center of the circle. Begin this practice without the discus, but be sure to locate your right arm in the drag position before you begin any rotational movement. Regardless of whether you use the one and one-half or the one and three-quarters turn, concentrate on developing a one-to-pull count at the center of the circle. At the center of the circle, when your right foot hits, count one. When your left foot hits, count two. Then pull. This rhythmic count should help you to maintain the drag position of the discus, and prevent delivering the discus too early. If the discus is delivered too early, you will usually be thrown out of the circle to the right of 12 o'clock.

During your fourth unit of practice develop a recovery from the reverse. The reverse occurs after the discus has left your hand. During the delivery your body is travelling at high speed in a rotational course. As the discus leaves your hand, your arm reacts by flexing toward the center of rotation. This movement establishes a momentary increase in speed that must be brought under control. Extending the right arm as soon as possible will assist in slowing rotation.

When both feet have returned to the surface of the circle and you have complete control of your body, walk out the rear half of the circle.

Each unit of practice has brought you to a point where you should now be ready to execute a complete throw under maximum control. Remember that the first part of the discus turn is used to develop speed for the final delivery. Loss of body control at any time before you arrive at the center of the circle will only tend to compound your errors.

COUNTDOWN

When you enter the circle for a competitive or practice throw, review the basic moves you are about to execute:

1. Is the discus in proper grip position?
2. Are my feet properly located in the circle?
3. Will my shoulders and hips be back when I start rotation?
4. Will I locate my arm in the drag position?
5. Will I remember to exercise control over my speed when I turn?
6. When I hit the center of the circle, will I explode into the throw?
7. When I complete the throw, will I walk out the rear half of the circle?

SAFETY PRECAUTIONS

If no protective screen is provided, never throw the discus when another person is on the release side of the circle. Never throw without ascertaining that the landing sector is clear. The safety of anyone in the general area of the discus circle is your responsibility.

If your discus becomes damaged, replace or repair it immediately. Chips or burrs along the blade edge can cause serious injury to your fingers, so sand them down before you continue to throw. Loose screws in the metal plates on the side of the discus are extremely dangerous. Keep a clean towel available at the circle whenever you are throwing. Keep your hands clean and dry to help prevent the discus from slipping out of your hand. Loose dirt can cause a bad spill during a turn, so keep a broom available to sweep the circle.

CHAPTER 10

THE SHOT PUT

The shot put is an event in which a ball of metal, usually iron or brass, is projected through the air. The object is for the shot to travel as far as possible before striking the ground. The regulation weight of the ball is 12 pounds for high school competition and 16 pounds for college competition.

The surface from which the shot is put is usually cement or some other all-weather surface. Inscribed on the surface is a circle 7 feet in diameter. The circle is divided into front and rear halves by lines outside of and on each side of the circle. Located on the front half of the circle and occupying approximately 65° of the front half is a toe board 4 inches high and 4½ inches wide. The landing area for the shot is level with the throwing surface and bound by lines passing from the exact center of the circle along the side of the toe board to the limits of any possible throw.

You will begin shot putting by learning to grip the ball properly. Then you will learn the proper stance. Next, you will learn the glide movement. Finally, you will learn the progression of movement from the rear to the front of the circle.

THE GRIP

There are three generally accepted grips for this event. It is suggested that you try each of them and select the one you find most comfortable for use.

In all three grips, proper positioning of the ball on your hand is extremely important. It is important, too, that you do not attempt to grip the ball too high on your fingers because of the strong possibility of finger strain. Although later in your training you may position the ball higher on your fingers, during this stage of training the ball should always be in contact with the base of your fingers.

From this point on, the directions are for a right-handed shot putter.

To take the first grip, place the ball on the ground. Spread your fingers in a normal position and grasp the ball in your right hand. When all five fingers enclose the ball, and the area of the base of your fingers is in contact with the ball, pick it up. Do not permit your palm to contact the ball. Raise the ball to shoulder level, permitting your elbow to position directly under the weight of the ball. If the ball should begin to slip into the palm of your hand, exert pressure with your fingers. This act should help maintain the ball in proper position. In this position, your thumb and little finger provide lateral support, while the other fingers provide a base behind the ball. Now, let your wrist bend slightly to the rear. This position will provide greater wrist flexion during the put.

Shot put grip No. 1.

The second style for gripping the ball may be attempted by bringing the ball to the same shoulder level position as described above. At this position, curl your little finger under the ball so as to provide a broad lateral base opposite your thumb. The broad base opposite your thumb may provide you with more stability in your grip. Your other three fingers, again, provide a base behind the ball.

Shot put grip No. 2.

The third grip is arrived at in the same manner as the other two. However, when the ball is brought to shoulder level, the four fingers are placed more directly behind the ball and the thumb is brought to a position almost opposite the fingers. Very little lateral stability is provided in this position, and the grip is usually reserved for more accomplished shot putters.

Shot put grip No. 3.

Regardless of the grip you select, the degree of control you exercise over the ball will be the most important consideration. Only after you have attempted a number of puts will you be able to make a final selection. Don't be in a hurry to settle on a grip.

THE CARRYING POSITION

This is the position in which you will maintain the ball at all times up to the actual put. You will not initiate any action until the ball is placed in this position, and you will maintain it as you progress from the rear of the circle to the front of the circle. The carrying position is critical because it maintains the ball in proper relation to the rest of your body as you drive across the circle.

Pick up the ball in whichever grip you choose. Now, cradle it against your neck, slightly below your jaw bone, being sure to maintain pressure against your neck. Keep your elbow below the weight of the ball. Do not cramp your arm against your body. Let it hang loose in the support position. If it is more comfortable to hold your elbow slightly away from your body, this is permissible.

Carrying position of shot.

LEAD-UP SKILLS

Shot putting is learned first in the standing position. Since your position in the shot circle must always be considered in relation to the landing area, you must always orient your body in relation to that area. For this reason, you should consider the circle to be similar to the face of a clock placed on the ground. The desired direction of throw is to the center of the landing sector. Call this 12 o'clock. The rear of the circle is 6 o'clock. The line from 6 o'clock to 12 o'clock will be your base line of reference.

Remember that for further discussion, when movement along the base line is considered, 3 o'clock and 9 o'clock are always at right angles to the base line.

As you prepare for a standing throw, face 3 o'clock and place your right foot at the center of the circle with your toe pointed toward 4 o'clock. Place your left foot to the rear, in the direction of 12 o'clock, with your left toe located in the direction of 2 o'clock.

Grip the ball in your desired style and place it in the carrying position. Now, rotate your shoulders so your left shoulder points in the direction of 3 o'clock and your right in the direction of 9 o'clock. Flex your right knee and permit your weight to shift to the ball of your right foot. From a vertical position, bend at your waist 15° so as to incline your chest toward the ground at the back of the circle. Raise your left arm to shoulder level with your elbow pointed toward the rear of the circle. Bend your elbow so your forearm is at right angles to the base line and level with your chest. Your head and eyes should be facing to the rear. You are now in position for a standing put.

Shot putter in standing position at center of circle.

Your put will begin when you press your right foot onto the ground by extending your right knee. This action will initiate forward and upward rotation of your right hip. If you exert enough pressure against the ground, your weight will be transferred to your left foot as your hip comes to a position at right angles to the base line. Your left leg, which has been slightly flexed, extends as it accepts the weight of your body, and your left elbow should be rotated forcefully to the rear. The ball, which has been cradled to your neck through the action, is now driven up and away from the carrying position toward 12 o'clock. The desired angle of drive should be somewhere between 40° and 45°.

Coordination and continuity are the keys to success in the standing put. You must repeat the move again and again until it becomes a natural movement and on each effort you must execute the movement from start to finish as a single flowing process. Since almost 90 per cent of your total distance will be obtained from the standing position, perfection of this move must be mastered before the complete throw is attempted.

ADVANCED TECHNIQUES

The advanced put begins at the rear of the circle. Place your right foot along the base line with your toe pointed toward 6 o'clock. Place your left foot to the rear, along the base line, in the direction of 12 o'clock. Point your left toe toward 2 o'clock. With most of your weight supported on the ball of your right foot, establish a light balance contact with your left foot. Your hips and shoulders should be at right angles to the base line and your left arm should be located in the same position you established at the center of the circle in the standing put.

Shot putter at rear of circle ready to glide.

Action is initiated by lifting your left foot from the circle while your right knee is flexed. Next, your left leg is extended toward 12 o'clock as your right leg extends. This action results in movement toward the center of the circle. As your right foot leaves the ground, it must be turned slightly so as to land pointing toward four o'clock at the center of the circle. Prior to the landing of your right foot, you must flex your knee in order to be ready to drive your hip forward

Side view of beginning of glide. Left foot moving.

Right leg under body at conclusion of glide.

and up. When you complete your landing, the action that follows is the same as that described in the standing put.

Because of the increased speed generated from the glide, your body will tend to continue moving forward after the shot is released. As your weight moves onto your left foot for the put, drag your right foot forward until it approaches the position occupied by your left foot. After the ball has been released, and before your right leg touches your left, quickly pull your left foot to the rear and place your right foot on the ground with your toe pointing in the direction of 11 o'clock. Your right foot absorbs the shock of your forward movement and prevents your body from moving past the toe board. This movement is called the reverse.

PRACTICE SESSIONS

The following suggestions for practice may be helpful. From them, the beginner may be able to organize his work-out, and a more advanced shot putter may find a method for improving a particular part of his technique. While a progression from unit to unit should be followed by a beginning shot putter, a more advanced athlete

CORRECTION CHART

Error	Causes	Corrections
1. High delivery, no distance.	a. Elbow too close to body.	a. Move elbow farther from body to the approximate angle at which you plan to deliver ball.
	b. Premature hip rotation and late delivery.	b. Organize movements in your mind: foot, knee, hip, arm.
	c. Weight not transferred to left foot prior to delivery.	c. Do not deliver the ball until your weight has moved to your left foot.
	d. Elbow moving ahead of chest after weight transfer.	d. Keep elbow behind ball.
2. Low delivery, no distance.	a. Elbow lifted during glide.	a. Maintain stable position of elbow during glide.
	b. Failure to lift under the ball with right or left leg.	b. Initiate movement at the center of the circle with right leg extension.
		c. Extend left leg during the release.
3. Normal delivery, no distance.	a. Rear leg in the extended position during landing at the center of the circle.	a. When gliding from rear of circle draw rear foot quickly under your body.
	b. Movements not occurring in proper sequence.	b. Foot, knee, hip, arm sequence must occur in that order.
	c. Premature release of shot.	c. Extend left arm completely before releasing the shot.

may, with good purpose, organize his own progression using those suggestions that seem to meet his particular need in technique development.

Primarily, shot put practice sessions are used to improve your techniques. Occasionally, they are used to test your ability prior to competition. Each practice session or unit, made up of a series of sessions, should have a specific purpose. You may be attempting to improve the position of your right leg during the glide, or you may be attempting to maintain the shot in the proper carrying position until

CORRECTION CHART *(Continued)*

Error	Causes	Corrections
4. Shot landing to the right side of sector.	a. Late rotation of right hip.	a. Wait until your hips are at right angles to direction of throw before putting.
	b. Early delivery of right arm.	b. Shoulders rotated too far to the rear when putting action begins.
	c. Improper foot position at center of circle.	c. Check to see that right foot is landing in a position with toe pointed toward 4 o'clock.
5. Shot landing to the left side of sector.	a. Early rotation of right hip.	a. Check to see that right foot is not landing pointed too far toward 12 o'clock.
	b. Late release of shot.	b. Release the shot toward 12 o'clock.
	c. Too much left arm drive to rear before shot release begins.	c. Coordinate right hip rotation with left arm drive.
6. Loss of shot control during release.	a. Fingers too close together.	a. Spread fingers more.
	b. Shot moving off neck during glide.	b. Hold ball firm against neck and maintain that position until right hip comes to 3 o'clock position.
	c. Right elbow moving under ball during glide.	c. Maintain elbow at planned angle of flight position during glide and landing.

the last critical moment. Whatever your purpose, you may have to concentrate through a single work-out or a series of work-outs until you have mastered the problem. Learn to practice in units reaching a specific goal before moving on to the next problem.

For the first unit of practice, disregard the circle until you have attempted the three possible grips. Hold the ball in the carrying position and toss it away. Do not at this point concern yourself with foot or leg position. When you feel you have become familiar with one of the grips, move to the center of the circle. Grip the shot properly. Place it in the carrying position and adjust your body for a stand-ing throw. Your goal for this unit will be to initiate movement from the flexed knee position of your right leg.

You may find that it will assist your concentration to look down at your right knee as you prepare to practice the movement. Extend your leg and push your foot against the ground. The resulting action will cause your right hip and shoulder to move upward. Repeat the movement until you are satisfied that this initiates movement. You must first learn to move the ball upward at the center of the circle. Next, add the rotation of your right foot. Again, it may be helpful to watch the movement take place. Your knee must begin extending before the rotation of the foot takes place. Do not put the shot. Maintain it in the carrying position at all times. Repeat the movement 10 or 15 times until you have the "feel" of the movement. Your purpose is to cause the large leg muscles to overcome the inertia of the shot. Do not move to the next unit until you can effect the proper leg action. Be sure during this unit to practice to maintain the rearward position of the hips and shoulders and the proper placement of your left foot.

When you have mastered the first unit, move on to unit two. Your purpose will now be to develop the rotational movement of your right hip. As your right leg extends and the foot rotates, your left hip is driven toward 12 o'clock. As the weight of your body moves onto your left foot, it must provide resistance to movement beyond the foot. In effect, the left leg and foot "block" against the ground at the instant your weight has shifted completely onto them. With your left foot resisting the movement of the left side of your body, your center of gravity will shift slightly in that direction. This shift will help attain a closer and therefore more rapid rotation of your right hip about your center of gravity.

When your weight has shifted from the right to left foot, you have completed all the effective rotation needed for the put. Your hips and shoulders are now at right angles to the base line of reference, your left knee is slightly flexed, and you are ready to lift into the weight of the ball. Your left knee extends and the ball is pushed from the carrying position into the proper flight path.

During this stage of training some beginning shot putters tend to develop two possible bad habits. Either they throw before they have completed the weight transfer to their left leg, or, having transferred, they quickly draw their left hip to the rear, causing them to fall backward onto their right foot before the lift is completed. The counter-movement of your left hip will reduce or negate the forward rotation of your right hip. To some degree, keeping the left knee flexed until your body weight has moved over this leg will help solve this problem. If, when you have completed your movement, you find that your weight is over your right foot and you have fallen slightly to the rear, have a partner observe the action of your left hip at the release point.

Your third unit of practice should concern itself with lifting the shot away from the carrying position. In general, you should attempt to approximate an angle of 45°.

Many beginning shot putters attempt to move the ball at a very low angle. The fault is the result of poor timing in the coordinated lift, or in the concept of attaining high lift. Try placing a high jump cross-bar about 6 feet off the ground at a distance two-thirds of the way toward your best throwing mark. Attempt to throw the ball over the cross-bar. In order to accomplish this result, the ball must be close to its highest point half-way toward the point at which it should land. You will have to lift the ball higher during the release in order to obtain cross-bar clearance.

In your fourth unit, you may wish to concern yourself with the reverse. If you are having trouble remaining within the circle after the release, now is the time to correct your error.

Most often, failure to remain in the circle is the result of two faults: (1) Failing to coordinate the release action. Beginning shot men will sometimes tend to delay the release until their body is well beyond the left foot. In this case, rather than providing lift, the left foot is pushing them out of the circle. (2) Failing to drag the right foot and leg toward the front of the circle. Beginners will sometimes tend to throw the right knee forcefully forward and up. This indicates a failure to shift onto the left leg and produces an overbalance forward, resulting in a foul.

Until you have mastered the techniques of the standing throw, it is not wise to practice the glide. If your standing technique is incorrect, the added speed of the glide will only tend to compound your errors. However, when you feel you are ready to move to the rear of the circle, it is time to move to unit five.

Execution of the glide was described earlier under "advanced techniques." Before moving to the circle, find a flat area and, without the shot, position yourself for an advanced put. Execute the glide movement a few times, coming to a stop when both feet return to the ground. Observe your foot placement upon landing. Continue this practice until you establish proper position. Then, attempt to continue through a series of gliding movements. Glide toward 12 o'clock; land with your toes pointed toward 4 o'clock; push off; glide to a foot placement toward 6 o'clock; push off; glide to a foot placement toward 4 o'clock; and continue for as many glides as your balance control will permit.

This process of continuous glides will help develop your foot and leg action while requiring proper body balance. If during this process you do not bring your right leg back to a flexed landing position, you will not be able to maintain balance or thrust into the next glide. Repeat this practice until you are able to execute six or seven continuous glides. Then, use the shot in the drill. Place it in the carrying position and execute a series of glides. Have a partner observe whether the shot remains in the proper carrying position during each of the glides.

Control over the action and position of your left arm will be important during this drill. The left arm must remain in a balanced, passive position, level with the shoulders and at right angles to the base line of reference. Failure to maintain this position will result in premature upper body rotation. Proper positioning will help maintain the hips and shoulders at right angles to the base line of reference during the glide.

When you have mastered the glide drill outside the circle, move to the circle and attempt a single glide and throw. Do not attempt to throw hard or far. Practice to attain good balance control and acceleration from the rear to the front of the circle. As your technique improves, attempt to gain more speed, but not at the cost of balance control.

While each part of the shot put movement is in some way independent, you must finally work for an action that is coordinated and, above all, that produces a continuity of movement from the rear to the front of the circle. Continuity is developed when you practice the complete movement. As you practice toward your final goal, attempt to establish a quick, relaxed movement. The more intense and exacting your practice sessions are, the more relaxed your competitive put will probably be. Controlled relaxation promotes speed and proper execution.

COUNTDOWN

When you finally begin to compete, develop a routine that will prepare you for your best effort. As you stand in the circle preparing to throw, ask yourself these questions:

1. Is the shot properly located in my hand?
2. Have I established the proper carrying position?
3. Is my right foot properly located and positioned?
4. Is my left foot in position?
5. When I move, what will be my sequence of movements?
6. When I have completed the put, what will be my sequence of movements?

Remember that when you do move, you must coordinate all your actions and they must terminate in an explosive movement of the ball, up and away.

SAFETY PRECAUTIONS

The shot is not easily damaged; however, it can become nicked or dented from striking stones or other hard objects. To prevent injury to your hand from nicks or dents, sand down any sharp edges.

Maintain the surface of the circle in the best possible condition. Sweep it clean before each attempted put to prevent slipping.

To insure a secure, safe grip on the ball, keep the ball as dry as possible during rainy weather and keep your hands dry at all times.

Finally, never throw the shot when people are in the landing area.

CHAPTER 11

THE HIGH JUMP

The high jump, or running high jump, as it should be more correctly called, has been a competitive event in track and field for about 80 years. During this period, four different styles of jumping have evolved, and at present, a fifth style is being tried and tested.

The high jump pit should have a minimum dimension of 16 feet wide by 12 feet deep. It should be deep enough and of such a composition that it will provide a completely safe and comfortable landing.

The high jump runway should have at least 50 feet of level and unvarying surface from any angle within an arc of 180°.

The distance between the vertical uprights shall not be less than 12 feet or more than 13 feet 2.25 inches. The cross-bar shall rest between the uprights and be of wood, metal, or other suitable material, triangular or circular in shape.

In high jumping, you are challenged with the problem of converting horizontal movement to vertical movement. In order to accomplish the conversion, one foot is set firmly against the ground ahead of your body, and the other foot is swung as rapidly as possible above the cross-bar. Your body is lifted off the ground by the momentum of your lead leg and the push of your rear leg. After the take-off you must place your body in the flattest possible position as it crosses the bar, or curl your body so that each portion will pass over the bar when it is at the highest point above the ground and over the bar. Your landing is usually a matter of simply dropping into a soft pit of rubber, sawdust, or some other material that will absorb shock.

As stated earlier, there are four established jumping styles. They are known as the scissors, the Eastern roll, the Western roll and the straddle. Of these, only the straddle is used extensively by present day high jumpers; however, the other three will be discussed briefly to provide a foundation for understanding the problems that a high jumper must solve in propelling his body up and over the cross-bar.

The Scissor

This style of jumping depends on a fast approach and a forceful kick-up of the leg near the bar. The jumper clears the bar in the seated position and lands on the foot of the kick-up leg. The scissor style jumper faces three problems: (1) passing over the bar in the seated position requires the center of gravity to be lifted higher than in other styles; (2) the high speed approach required for clearance does not permit ample time to convert momentum upward, and (3) in order to accomplish the landing on the lead foot, it must be brought up and down in rapid succession. While the jumper is in the air, these movements are not compatible.

The Eastern

In the Eastern roll, the approach is almost straight at the bar. The lead leg is kicked upward and, as it passes over the bar, the rear leg is brought under the body and above the cross-bar. This action results in a rotation of the body, which turns the jumper so he is facing down toward the bar as it is cleared. In contrast to the scissors, this style permits a lay-out position, which is more effective. However, two major problems are common: (1) the high angle of approach requires a take-off well away from the bar and considerable effort is expended traveling a long distance in the air, and (2) the underside tuck of the rear leg means that the center of gravity must be projected higher to allow clearance for the leg to pass over the bar.

The Western

The Western roll is accomplished by approaching the cross-bar from an angle of less than 45°. The leg nearer the bar plants against the ground, and the outside leg is kicked up above the bar. As the high point over the bar is attained, the rear leg is pulled to a position between the body and the cross-bar. The jumper is lying on his side as he crosses the bar.

While the approach angle of the Western roll provides a more efficient position for changing direction in front of the bar, a single important problem still exists: The lay-out position of the body with the trail leg between the cross-bar and the lead leg requires added height over the bar.

The Straddle

The straddle roll is the most common style of jump used because it permits the most efficient change of direction at the take-off and lay-out clearance over the cross-bar. The angle of approach to the bar is less than 45° and the foot nearer the bar is placed against the ground as the outside leg is swung upward. As the body moves upward, the shoulders are turned toward the bar so the chest faces the ground during the clearance. The upward swing of the lead leg is coordinated with the push of the trail leg. The body crosses the bar in a lay-out position with the face, shoulders, and hips all on the same plane, or with the head, then shoulders, then hips curling around the bar as they reach the highest point over the bar. The straddle jump permits the body to clear the bar with a minimum of wasted space. The weakness in the style comes in the necessity of dropping the shoulders toward the bar during the take-off, producing a downward rotation of the body.

The Fosbury Flop

The most recently evolved style is called the Fosbury Flop and is the product of the efforts of Dick Fosbury, a young man who became an Olympic Champion. As yet, the Fosbury style has not become generally accepted as better than an individual style. Although effective for Fosbury, the style may prove useless for all but a few jumpers.

The Fosbury style calls for a rounding off approach immediately in front of the bar. The leg nearer the bar is kicked over the bar as the back is turned in the direction of the bar. At the highest point in the jump the athlete drops his head and shoulders toward the landing pit and executes a landing on his back.

An important consideration in the Fosbury style landing is the depth and softness of the landing pit. Recent medical studies have indicated that, unless the landing pit is properly constructed, there exists a danger of severe spinal damage during the landing. Unless your school provides the most modern equipment for high jumping, you should avoid the Fosbury style of jump.

Inasmuch as the straddle style jump still remains the most common form, further discussion will be related to the techniques of this style.

LEAD-UP SKILLS

There are many theories regarding the best way to begin high jumping. Your problem will be to attempt to take the primary attributes of each style and blend them into a final form. To begin, you must have some understanding of the factors working in your favor and how you can apply them.

The first factor is speed: if it is controlled and used properly, speed can assist in getting you high off the ground. The second is strength: when applied quickly, strength can help you attain proper body position and lift. The third is coordination: it can bring about the most effective use of all other attributes.

During further discussion we will consider you to be right-handed.

Place a cross-bar about 2 feet above the ground on the high jump standard. Position yourself at the mid-point of the bar with your right shoulder in the direction of the bar and your body an arm's length away.

Place a scratch or chalk mark on the ground in front of your right toe. Next, with a partner observing your step pattern, begin with a left step and run three steps away from the cross-bar on an angle of 45°. Have your partner mark the landing of your third step.

Turn about. Stand with both feet over your third step landing point and run toward the bar again, beginning with a left step. Have your partner observe your step pattern and, as your left foot strikes the ground on the third step, swing your right leg forward and up over the bar in the line of your approach. Push off with your left foot and, as you leave the ground, rotate your right shoulder in the direction of the bar.

At a low height, your landing in the pit will usually occur on your right foot because there is no need to lower your upper body toward the bar in order to clear the height.

Your partner, who observed your approach and jump, should now inform you whether your left foot landed on the take-off point. If your step pattern carried you beyond the mark closer to the bar, move your starting mark back a distance equal to the over-step. If your take-off occurred before the mark nearer the bar, move your starting mark closer to the bar a distance equal to the under-step. By repeating this approach routine a few times, you can quickly establish an exact take-off position. It is important that you learn to avoid looking at the take-off mark close to the bar because any movement of the head in a downward direction will result in downward rotation at the moment of take-off.

Once you have established a constant approach pattern, you can begin developing high jump techniques.

Move to the starting point of your approach and walk through the following step pattern. Begin with a normally coordinated left step forward. Continue forward toward your right foot placement and, as you do so, swing both arms forward and away from your body so that your hands are about waist high and beginning to move toward the rear when your right foot strikes the ground. Continue the rearward movement of your arms as you continue to your left foot placement. The rearward movement of your arms will make your body incline slightly to the rear and your left step occur in advance of your center of gravity (located in your hip area). As your left step strikes the ground, your body should be inclined rearward and your arms should be completing a circular movement, which now positions them parallel to your body and pointed directly toward the ground. The rotational movement of your arms is continued forward and is coordinated with the upward kick of your right leg. As your right leg moves upward, your body weight will be passing over your left foot. You must now attempt to coordinate the upward movement of your right leg with an extension of your left leg and ankle so that maximum lift is provided to your body.

Waist-high arm position of high jumper.

Arms to rearward prior to take-off.

Repeat this walk-through process until you have attained a high degree of coordination in the movements. Then, attempt to run through the movements at a slow pace. Concentrate on proper timing and a forceful lift of the right leg with an extension of the left leg.

During the walk-through process you should have been able to clear the cross-bar with little effort. As you increase your approach speed, you should jump well above the 2-foot height at which the cross-bar has been set. Raise the bar to a height of 3 feet and continue jumping with your lead-up skills.

ADVANCED TECHNIQUES

The advanced techniques of high jumping include increased approach speed, lowering the upper half of the body to a lay-out position during clearance of the cross-bar, and a lay-out landing in the pit.

Greater approach speed is attained by increasing the number of steps taken toward the cross-bar. Four preliminary steps are used to develop speed and arrive at the mark from which the lead-up skills were practiced. Hereafter we will refer to this point as a "check mark." As you approach this check mark, your right foot must land beside it, so that you will arrive at your take-off point properly positioned in relation to the cross-bar.

Start of high jump approach. Left foot moving past check mark.

If desired, a second check mark can be established at the beginning of the four preliminary steps, using the same method that established the lead-up pattern.

The lay-out position is attained by lowering the upper half of your body to the same level as your hips when they reach maximum height above the ground. As your left foot leaves the ground during the take-off, your right shoulder is rotated inward toward the bar. At this point, every effort must be made to bring your hips as high as possible, while lowering your upper body as little as possible, to attain the lay-out position. At the moment of cross-bar clearance your body should be parallel to the bar or crossing the bar as each part reaches the highest point above the bar.

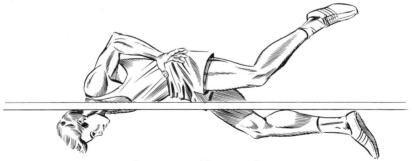

Lay-out position over bar.

The lay-out landing is the product of controlled approach speed, proper take-off, and relaxed cross-bar clearance. The body rotation you established while leaving the ground should result in your landing either on your right side or completely on your back.

The approach

The high jump approach can be accomplished using any desired number of steps. However, seven-step patterns usually prove most effective for beginners.

Either one or two check marks can be used to attain proper placement of the take-off foot. Skilled jumpers can use one check mark located at the beginning of their approach, but beginners should use a mark closer to the cross-bar so as to reduce the possible error in take-off placement.

The speed of your approach is the most critical factor to be considered. If you approach too fast, your body will pass over your take-off foot before it is able to provide the desired coordination with the lead foot. If you approach too slowly, you will not attain sufficient momentum to lift you to the greatest possible height.

During the last three steps of your approach, you must attain proper body position. Each of your last three steps should be slightly longer than the previous step so as to lower your center of gravity before the take-off. Your last step must be executed with your heel striking the ground first and your knee flexing slightly as your weight transfers forward to the ball of your foot. During this weight transfer, your trail foot is swung forcefully forward and up in a coordinated movement with your arms.

The take-off

Your take-off occurs directly over your left foot and at the most vertical angle possible. The tempo of your right leg must be increased into the jump so as to convert horizontal movement into vertical movement before momentum is lost.

As your lead foot reaches the highest point in its upward movement, it is turned toward the cross-bar and suspended in that position until your hips lift to the same plane. Your upper body must be lowered to the same plane as your center of gravity in order to produce a lay-out position.

Cross-bar clearance

As your upper body comes level with the cross-bar, your left arm is drawn close to your chest and your right arm is dropped over and around the cross-bar. Your lead foot should then be dropped directly toward the landing pit as your trail foot and leg rotate up and away from the bar. It is important to avoid any kicking action of the trail foot at this moment if your body is to continue to rotate around the axis of the cross-bar with your face, chest, and abdomen facing the bar. A kicking action will slow rotational speed and cause your foot to knock the bar off the standard.

CORRECTION CHART

Error	Causes	Corrections
1. Kicking bar with lead foot.	a. Take-off foot too close to cross-bar.	a. Adjust check marks.
2. Landing far behind cross-bar.	a. Take-off too far in front of cross-bar.	a. Adjust check marks.
		b. Execute heel landing of take-off foot so as to increase lift and reduce forward movement during take-off.
3. Lack of lift during take-off.	a. Not enough speed during approach.	a. Adjust speed to permit maximum controlled approach.
	b. Failure to place take-off foot in advance of center of gravity.	b. Arms must be dropped to the rear of body before take-off foot strikes ground.
	c. Incomplete lift of lead leg during take-off.	c. When take-off foot strikes the ground, swing the rear foot forward and up.
	d. Lack of knee flexion following landing of take-off foot.	d. Execute heel landing of take-off foot and roll to the ball of your foot while your knee bends.
	e. Lack of arm lift.	e. When your lead leg begins to move upward, your arms should be swinging forward and up.
4. Lack of rotation around the cross-bar.	a. Failure to establish rotation before leaving the ground.	a. Turn your take-off foot slightly toward the bar when it lands. Follow with shoulders.
5. Hitting cross-bar with trail knee or foot.	a. Kicking or extending the trail leg while over the cross-bar.	a. After leaving the ground, maintain the rear leg in a stable position.
6. Hitting cross-bar with the inside of arm nearer the bar.	a. Not bringing the arm close to the body following the take-off.	a. As the arm nearer the bar is lifted into the jump, bring your hand in toward your chest.

The landing

If the jump is properly executed, your landing will occur on your right side or back. When you contact the pit, relax and permit the material to absorb the shock of your landing. Do not attempt to bounce out of the pit, as this action can dislodge the bar or cause injury if you do not have your balance when you return to the ground.

PRACTICE SESSIONS

High jump practice sessions are usually devoted to varied activities. You might try running, weight lifting, skipping rope, and practice approaches concluded with a high kick. During the last activity, no attempt is made to clear the cross-bar; you jump vertically as high as possible and kick high into the air. The landing is made on the take-off foot. This practice movement helps develop rhythm and vertical take-off.

During your first unit of practice you should develop a three-step approach and clearance. Until you are able to jump from a desired take-off point, you should not attempt to jump for height.

Your second unit of practice must be concerned with proper foot placement, body angle, and arm action. You must slowly begin to develop the unnatural arm swing used in the high jump take-off. Until this pattern of movement can be well coordinated, no attempt should be made to increase the height of the cross-bar.

Your third unit may be used to learn the complete approach run and more vigorous arm and leg action. During this unit you must also become concerned with the lowering of the upper body during cross-bar clearance.

Your fourth unit can be concerned with development of the fine techniques of jumping: left arm position, lead leg drop, and rear leg clearance.

Bear in mind that a unit is not a single day's practice, but rather the complete learning of all the skills in a progression to the final advanced technique. A unit may last a day or a week depending on your needs and your ability to master fundamental skills.

COUNTDOWN

Whenever your prepare to execute a jump, ask yourself a routine set of questions related to the movements you are about to attempt.

1. Are my check marks properly established?
2. How can I attain a rhythmic approach?

3. On my take-off step, what will assist in producing greater lift?

4. What must I do when my body reaches the cross-bar?

5. How can I improve my clearance of the cross-bar?

6. If I am in competition, what is my present status in relation to other competitors?

SAFETY PRECAUTIONS

The most dangerous areas related to the high jump are the landing pit and the approach surface.

The landing pit must be kept soft at all times if it is not a modern soft rubber material. If sawdust or sand is used, care must be taken to maintain the pit in the best possible condition. It must be frequently turned in order to permit air drying, and it must be kept free of foreign materials that cause injury during the landing.

The approach area must be consistent in quality. If it is made of a hard material, you must keep it well swept and free of foreign objects. If it is soft, dirt or grass, you must attempt to keep it as level as possible. So called "housekeeping" around the high jump area will usually reward you with better results. Anything you do to improve the area will improve your jumping.

CHAPTER 12

THE TRIPLE JUMP

The triple jump is a relative newcomer to the American track and field scene. Until recently, American athletes competed in the event only during the Olympic year. Today it is found in almost all programs and at every level of competition. At one time this event was referred to by Americans as the "hop-step-and-jump." Now we use the Olympic designation of triple jump.

In execution, the event includes three movements. The first movement is a hop in which the take-off and landing occur on the same foot. The second movement is a step with the landing on the opposite foot. The third movement is a jump with the landing on both feet. The pattern of steps would appear like this:

$$\frac{}{R} \quad \frac{}{R} \quad \frac{L}{} \quad \frac{L}{R} \quad \text{or} \quad \frac{L}{} \quad \frac{L}{} \quad \frac{}{R} \quad \frac{L}{R}$$

The most effective triple jump is accomplished by maintaining speed during all the movements and attaining slightly more height as you progress through each separate movement.

LEAD-UP SKILLS

Before any attempt is made to execute a hard jump, the basic foot pattern of movements must be learned.

From this point on, the directions are for a jumper executing the first hop on his right foot.

Stand with both feet together. Execute one initial step with your left foot in order to gain momentum. Now continue your movement with the placement of your right foot on the ground. Hop into the air from your right foot and land on your right foot. Next step forward with your left foot, land on it, and jump into the air. Land on both feet, side by side.

Repeat these movements until they become natural. Do not attempt to travel more than 3 or 4 feet on each separate move. When you feel you are able to execute the triple jump with a reasonable degree of confidence, move to the long jump or triple jump area and place a mark on the runway about 15 feet from the landing pit; place a second mark 10 feet from the pit, and a third mark 5 feet from the pit. Now position yourself on the runway and begin running toward the first mark. Adjust your stride so as to arrive at the first mark on your right foot. Hop into the air and land on the second mark with your right foot. Step forward with your left foot onto the third mark, jump into the air, and land in the pit about 5 feet from the edge.

The total distance of this jump is about 20 feet, and this should be enough to help you attain a sense of the jumping rhythm and the footwork involved. When you are able to execute the footwork with ease, you may increase the spacing between marks. While the exact spacing of your marks will depend on your individual strengths and weaknesses, a good general rule is to estimate your total desired distance and cover 35 per cent on the hop, 30 per cent on the step, and 35 per cent on the jump. While you are still jumping easily attainable distances, you can plot these percentages on the runway and attempt to hit each mark exactly. When you move to the advanced jump, do not use plot marks on the runway, as they will interfere with your concentration on the techniques of the jump.

Hereafter, the various movements of the triple jump will be identified by their "old" names: hop, step, and jump.

ADVANCED TECHNIQUES

During your beginning jumps, you have not attempted to gain great distance or speed. As you move into the advanced jump, you must be aware of the factors that will produce the best jumps.

THE APPROACH RUN AND JUMP

The minimum length of the triple jump runway is 130 feet. Located on the runway, flush with the surface, is a take-off board 8 inches wide and 4 feet long. The edge of the take-off board nearer to the landing pit is the scratch or foul line. During the approach run you must hit the established check marks so as to arrive at the take-off board on proper stride and in position to avoid a foul. (Review the method for attaining check marks in the long jump chapter.) Through the entire run you should be attempting to maintain even strides and body control. As you reach the take-off board, you must place your foot under your center of gravity and run outward and upward off the board. This body positioning permits you to leave the take-off board with a relatively flat trajectory and a minimum loss of speed.

Your left leg is driven forward and upward to a position similar to a normal running stride. Your arms are carried in a relatively relaxed manner and their primary function is to coordinate with your leg action for balance.

Right foot position during take-off.

In the hop, you must attempt to land with your right foot slightly forward of your center of gravity and attempt to pull back with your leg. The purpose of this is to maintain speed and give you time to lift your left knee to a higher level than in the hop. The added lift results in a slightly higher trajectory during the step movement. As your left leg lifts into the step, your right arm is moved forcefully forward in an uppercut as your left arm swings to the rear. Usually, your left knee will be lifted so that your thigh is parallel to the ground. The lower half of your left leg is vertical to the ground, your right thigh is vertical to the ground, and the lower portion of your right leg is parallel to the ground.

Body passing over right foot after hop landing.

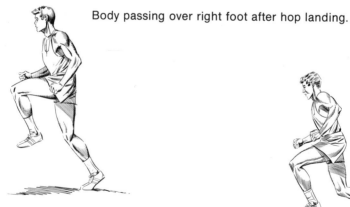

Body position in air during step flight.

Skilled triple jumpers attempt to attain what is called "suspension" during this movement. In effect, they try to remain off the ground for a longer period by maintaining the flexed position of their legs until the last possible moment before the step landing occurs.

Just before your left foot strikes the ground, extend it forward and land on the heel. Your arms, moving in opposition balance with your legs, are permitted to lag slightly. When contact is completed by the ball of your left foot, the arms are forcefully coordinated into the jump movement. Your landing at the end of the step movement is similar to the long jump take-off. Your foot contacts the ground heel first in front of your center of gravity. As you roll forward onto the ball of your foot, your chest, head, and eyes are carried high as your center of gravity moves over the board. Then, as your left leg extends off the board, your right leg is driven forcefully upward into the take-off.

Body position immediately prior to step landing.

Take-off into jump phase.

During the flight through the air in the jump movement, you should execute a continued running action in the air. The duration of the running action should be one and one-half steps, ending with a side by side placement of your feet and an extension of your legs at the moment of landing. After the landing, you must avoid falling backward, or precious distance will be lost. (See the chapter on long jumping.)

Each movement of the triple jump demands continuity and body control. Speed must be maintained and each movement must produce a higher trajectory. The added height will help compensate for the natural loss of speed in each successive movement.

Since the success of each movement in the triple jump depends on the proper execution of the preceding movement, great care must be taken to initiate an efficient hop. If the trajectory of the hop is too high, you will strike the ground with more force than your leg can support at the landing. The result will be a downward movement of your body onto the left foot, producing a short step. At the conclusion of a well-executed hop and entry into the step, if you do not attain proper placement of your left foot upon landing you will not be able to produce a high trajectory jump. In the early movements of the triple jump, any error will be compounded through the following movements.

PRACTICE SESSIONS

Triple jump practice sessions are among the longest and most difficult in track and field. Your legs must be able to absorb the constant hard pounding that is inherent in the event. Therefore, you must begin practice early in the season. When you have attained good basic condition, divide your practice into units. Each unit should have a goal in the progression toward the final jump.

Your first unit should be used to learn the basic foot movements of the triple jump. Practice the footwork over short distances until you can execute each movement with a high degree of coordination. Slowly increase the distance you attempt to jump until you can jump a total of 30 feet with equal spacing of each move. You will probably be able to jump this distance relying totally on speed, with little concern for good technique. However, you must concentrate on technique, so reduce the speed of your approach and develop body control. Do not concern yourself with the take-off board during the first unit.

During your second unit, you should work on proper foot placement in relation to your body weight. A partner standing well to the side can help you understand your positions. On the hop, your body will be directly over your take-off foot, you will be almost in a vertical position as you leave the ground, and your arms will continue through normal coordinated movements. As you come to the landing at the end of the hop, reach your right foot slightly ahead of your body in order to permit time for your left leg to swing in a more upward course. On the step, you should execute more powerful coordinated arm movements before leaving the ground, and you must incline

CORRECTION CHART

Error	Causes	Corrections
1. Hop flight too high.	a. Placement of take-off foot too far ahead of center of gravity.	a. Take off directly over your foot.
	b. Excessive knee lift of lead leg.	b. Direct lead knee forward below level of hip.
2. Loss of speed upon landing after hop.	a. Failure to sweep foot toward the rear as landing occurs.	a. Before returning to the ground, begin moving foot toward the rear.
3. Step flight too low.	a. Collapse of weight over hop landing foot.	a. Do not attempt to obtain too much height on hop.
	b. Failure to lift knee during step take-off.	b. Raise knee to hip level during step take-off.
4. Jump take-off too low.	a. Lead foot not contacting ground in advance of center of gravity during step landing.	a. Reach foot forward before sweeping to rear after ground contact.
	b. Insufficient arm lift during take-off of jump.	b. Maintain arms in rearward position at conclusion of step phase of jump.
5. Falling to rear during landing of jump.	a. Improper body control during jump flight descent.	a. Maintain body in erect position at peak of jump flight.
6. Loss of body balance during any phase of flight.	a. Improper arm control.	a. Maintain arms slightly away from body from hop landing onward.
7. Short landing on hop, step, or jump.	a. Extending leg or legs toward ground during flight.	a. Maintain leg flexion during flight through air.
8. Any phase of complete jump either too long or too short.	a. Failure to maintain rhythm.	a. Attempt to maintain almost equal time spacing during each phase of the movements.

your upper body forward during your flight through the air. Body inclination helps maintain your legs off the ground and permits you to reach your foot farther in front of your center of gravity as you return to the ground.

On the jump, incline your body to the rear and attempt to lift your right knee high into the effort. You must thrust your head and chest upward, you must coordinate a powerful arm action, and you must attempt to delay contacting the ground for as long as possible by holding your feet up. Your body control through these movements must be developed through repeated efforts, first at slow speed then at increased speed, until you can attain maximum controlled speed and balance.

On your third unit, you can improve the approach run through use of check marks and you can begin increasing the spacing of your foot contacts after you leave the take-off board. You can attempt your most powerful movements at the greatest possible speed.

Periodically, you can incorporate a unit of rope skipping, first on one foot, then on the other, in order to help strengthen your legs and develop jumping rhythm; or you can practice jumping onto, from, or over a slightly raised platform for the same purpose.

Your fourth unit can be used to improve the trajectory of each take-off movement. One of the most critical errors made by beginning jumpers is the failure to produce lift at the beginning of the movement. If the trajectory of your flight becomes too high, the force with which you strike the ground will be too great for your legs to maintain proper support on landing. If the trajectory of your flight is too low, you will pass over your foot and leg before you can execute lifting movements. You must establish a medium effort related to your leg strength and leg speed. Only through repeated attempts will you be able to adjust to the right combination.

Some part of your practice periods must be concerned with attaining or improving effective jumping ratios for the various movements of the triple jump. Particular care must be taken to improve the step movement, which usually produces the poorest ratio for beginning jumpers. If, during your training, you find that your step movement is too short, immediately attempt to correct this point by looking for an error in your hop movement or knee lift into the step. Beginning jumpers will often fail to attain one-half of the required step distance.

COUNTDOWN

Before you attempt a jump, review the factors that will produce your best effort by asking yourself these questions.

1. Are my check marks properly located along the runway?

2. When I leave the take-off board, how can I control my trajectory?

3. What factors will affect my speed through the movements of the jump?

4. What factors will help improve my trajectory through each progressive movement of the total jump?

5. How can I attain effective jumping ratios?

SAFETY PRECAUTIONS

Triple jumping is a hard activity. Do not attempt prolonged efforts until you have properly trained your body to execute controlled movements.

Be sure that your footwear is proper for the surface from which you are jumping and wear protective heel pads during all training.

Keep a broom handy at the runway to sweep away the accumulation of loose sand or dirt that can cause your foot to slip during the take-off or landing movements.

Avoid jumping when you are tired. Your muscles must respond quickly and efficiently during the entire triple jump movement.

CHAPTER 13

THE LONG JUMP

The long jump is an event that requires two common qualities of most track and field events: basic speed and leg strength. The distance travelled in any jump is the result of how fast the jumper was travelling at the take-off and how high off the ground he carried his center of gravity.

The event itself can best be considered when divided into four parts: the run, the take-off, the action in the air, and the landing. Although simple in appearance, the long jump is no less complex than any field event, and for most athletes far more difficult to master than others.

LEAD-UP SKILLS

To begin learning the long jump, it is best not to use the take-off board, which is constructed of wood, is 8 inches wide and 4 feet long, and is set flush with the surface of the runway. Jumping without the take-off board will permit you to master the basic elements of the jump while not having to be concerned with an accurate placement of your take-off foot.

The run

The long jump run, also referred to as the approach, consists of a natural run from a distance in excess of 100 feet from the landing pit. The pit is an area of sand, or usually sand and sawdust, 9 feet wide, unlimited in length, and level with the runway. The purpose of the run is to attain maximum controllable speed at the take-off board or jump. To this end, a long jumper usually starts from a standing position at the end of the runway and attempts to build his speed as quickly as possible. In the final steps prior to the take-off, the jumper controls his speed in order to attain the most efficient possible position from which to execute the jump.

The take-off

The take-off is the most critical part of the long jump. Unless you have proper foot placement, leg lift, and body control, the jump will be less than your best. The take-off is accomplished through a four phase action: (1) a slight lateral shift of your weight over the take-off foot, (2) a slight lifting of your chest, head, and eyes, (3) a blocking action of your take-off foot, the result of a heel landing, and (4) a forceful lifting of your lead leg into the jump. Each of these actions must be achieved in proper sequence if a good take-off is to be accomplished.

Leg and body position as contact is made with take-off board.

The action in the air

The movements executed by a long jumper during flight through the air serve two purposes: they help maintain proper body balance, and they assist in attaining good body position for the landing. Your action in the air will depend on your choice of the two most common forms: the knee-tuck style or the hitch-kick style.

In the knee-tuck style, after you leave the ground, both knees are brought to the tuck position. This position is maintained until just before striking the pit, at which time both feet are extended ahead of your body to absorb the shock of the landing. The difficulty of this move lies in the problem of holding the legs in position for a long enough period of time. The pull of gravity usually causes the legs to drop too soon, resulting in a landing that occurs below the center of gravity rather than ahead of it.

Knee-tuck style during flight.

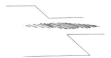

In the hitch-kick style, after you leave the ground, your legs continue a normal sequence of running action. The running action helps produce a more upright position of the body during flight. Your hips are therefore positioned slightly more forward than in the knee-tuck style, and you can execute a more efficient leg extension at the landing.

Hitch-kick style during flight.

The landing

As your body drops toward the landing surface, it is important that you resist depressing your trunk toward your thighs until the last instant before you extend your legs for the landing. At the moment of contact with the landing surface, your feet must be extended as far as possible in front of your body. It is important that you do not fall to the rear upon landing, because your jump will be measured from the point closest to the take-off board. When you hit the pit with your feet, attempt to thrust your chest forward as you permit your knees to flex. This action will help to carry your body weight over and beyond your feet.

Body position during landing of long jump.

You must practice the various parts of the beginning long jump until you have attained a reasonable degree of coordination and continuity of movement. Then you are ready to attempt jumping from the take-off board. The movements of jumping will be the same as you have practiced in your beginning jump, but the execution of the take-off must occur at an exact location on the runway.

ADVANCED TECHNIQUES

One of the primary problems to be resolved in the advanced jump is developing an approach run that will bring your jumping foot onto the take-off board in a natural running stride. To this end, check marks are established along the runway. From this point on, directions are for jumpers who take off from the right foot.

Check marks

Check marks are physical aids placed on or alongside the runway to assist you in establishing a fixed stride pattern to the take-off board. There may be two or more; however, two are generally used by most jumpers. If located alongside the runway, metal or wooden pins are usually used; if located on the runway, chalk lines or adhesive tape is most common.

Your check marks should have some easily identifiable characteristic. It may be color, size, or shape.

Check marks are established through a series of runs and readjustment. Place a mark 100 or more feet from the landing pit on the same side as your take-off foot. Next, move a few steps farther back along the runway and face in the direction of the take-off board.

At least one partner is required to help establish check marks. Have your partner stand in the area of the take-off board and observe the point where your take-off foot will land in relation to the board.

Check marks on runway.

From your position on the runway, begin running in the direction of the board and adjust your stride so your right foot lands exactly opposite the check mark. Continue your run beyond the board and into the pit. Consult with your partner, and locate the point where your right foot contacted the runway in the area of the take-off board. Mark the point and measure the distance to the take-off board. In relation to the first mark, if the point is beyond the board, add that distance to your run and relocate the first mark. If the point is short of the board, subtract that distance and relocate the first mark. Repeat the process until your right foot is contacting the board.

Now, have your partner stand about 40 feet from the board and locate a point on the runway where your right foot strikes. Place a second check mark here on the same side of the runway as your right foot. Having established the two check marks, return to the head of the runway and repeat the approach run. Be sure to contact the point opposite the check marks with your right foot and continue over and past the board with no attempt to adjust your stride in the area of the board.

Each time you execute an approach run, your partner must locate the landing point of your right foot near or on the take-off board and you must relocate both check marks as you did after your first run-through.

It will be important that you permit yourself enough rest between each approach run to start reasonably fresh. As fatigue begins to affect your run, there is a tendency for your stride to become erratic. Therefore, the number of approach runs must be limited by fatigue, or your check marks will constantly change.

In the beginning, be satisfied with any contact of your right foot on the take-off board. Minor variations in your stride will cause your foot placement on the board to shift forward or back. However, these changes can be readjusted and refined as you develop confidence in your approach run. Check marks are never exact. They must be readjusted in some small degree because of many factors, such as wind direction, weather conditions, runway conditions, and physical condition.

When you are satisfied that you have established check marks that are effective, begin running through and executing a take-off from the board. The process will be little different from your beginning jump routine.

PRACTICE SESSIONS

The number of jumps you can execute during any given practice session will be limited by many factors. Each session must be limited in light of your total physical condition, the length of your approach

CORRECTION CHART

Error	Causes	Corrections
1. Poor balance during take-off.	a. Excessive approach speed.	a. Control approach speed during last three strides.
2. Failure to attain height during take-off.	a. High center of gravity over take-off board.	a. Lower center of gravity during last two strides.
	b. Lack of knee lift during take-off.	b. Reduce approach speed so as to permit execution of basic jump movements. Roll from heel to ball of take-off foot and lift knee upward rather than forward.
	c. Incomplete thrust of rear leg.	c. Flex knee of jumping leg while passing over take-off board. Completely extend ankle of jumping leg as you leave the take-off board.
3. Loss of balance during flight.	a. Uncoordinated arm and leg action during take-off.	a. Maintain constant speed of body parts during take-off.
	b. Failure to take-off with center of gravity directly above take-off foot.	b. Shift body over take-off foot during last step.
	c. Arms carried too low during flight.	c. Permit arms to move away from your body for added balance.
4. Short landing in pit.	a. Dropping legs prematurely.	a. Hold legs up until just before landing. Attain vertical position of upper body during flight and delay forward lean until moment before landing. Do not look at pit during downward flight.
5. Falling to the rear after landing.	a. Legs too firm during landing.	a. When feet hit the pit, relax knees and roll forward.

run, and the number of approach runs required to refine your check marks.

A good method of practicing the important parts of the long jump without the use of a complete run-through is called "pops." During this form of practice you attempt to execute technically exact movements with a short approach run and jump. Pops allow you to practice a great many jumps before you become fatigued.

Usually, you do not practice pops from the take-off board because your approach speed is not normal and your body movements occur at a slower pace. Your purpose is to develop coordinated lift, balance in the air, and good landing techniques.

Establish a general take-off point on the runway close to the landing pit. Begin running from a point 30 or 40 feet from the take-off area and execute a jump incorporating your best skills. Concentrate upon an effective shift of the weight over your take-off foot, a heel landing, strong extension off the take-off leg, high knee lift of the lead knee, coordinated arm action, body control in the air, and effective landing.

The shift

During the step immediately preceding your take-off, your left foot is placed on the runway with your toes pointed slightly to the left. This foot positioning produces a push to the right as the stride is completed and the landing occurs on the right foot. Your center of gravity is therefore located more directly over your take-off foot as it executes the heel landing. This condition will help produce more effective upward lift through the remainder of the movement.

The heel landing

The heel landing occurs forward of your center of gravity and produces a slight lifting of your chest and head. At the same time, it permits you to begin lifting your lead knee into the jump. As your center of gravity passes over the take-off foot, the ball of the foot contacts the ground and permits a strong extension forward and up. During this action, your arms coordinate with your legs in a strong thrusting movement.

The arm action

The coordinated arm action is maintained until you reach the high point in the jump, at which time the arms are carried to the highest possible position above your head. This position is used to help sustain the high position of your legs during the downward flight. As the downward flight continues, your arms are lowered toward your feet to assist in countering the pull of gravity.

Body control

Your body control depends on the actions that have occurred immediately before the take-off. If you have attained good coordination, you will leave the ground in a relatively stable, vertical position, and there will be no need to make compensating movements in the air. If you have not attained coordination, these movements will occur in a natural attempt to maintain balance; however, they will detract from an efficient execution of the jump.

The landing

The effectiveness of your landing will also be related to each part of the jump occurring prior to its execution. As you attempt to sustain your feet until the last possible instant, press your upper body forward and down, rather than directly downward.

The organization of your practice units must be based on the progression of movements through the take-off and jump. Your first unit must be concerned with the run, the shift, and the heel landing. If you fail to shift properly, your normal foot placement on the next to the last stride will result in movement of your center of gravity away from your take-off placement. Have a partner stand directly ahead of or behind you during the shift execution. He can help you determine how much you are shifting.

If you fail to execute a heel landing, your center of gravity will pass over and beyond your take-off foot before your body can execute the movements necessary to provide lift.

When you have mastered the above parts of the jump, you can move to the second unit and develop strong arm thrust, knee lift, and take-off leg extension. Failure to attain these factors in the take-off will tend to produce low, ineffective jumping angles, or movements lacking the powerful thrust required in effective long jumping.

Your third unit of practice can be concerned with body control in the air and landing. These factors are closely related, and as already indicated are related to prior movements.

Your fourth unit is concerned with development of the approach run, use of check marks, and sprinting. As a prospective long jumper, you should be familiar with the techniques of sprinting, since much of your success will be related to the efficiency with which you approach at high speed.

During your fourth unit practice, when you practice the complete run and jump, you must constantly be aware that the most effective approach speed is a controlled run that will provide you the opportunity to execute the jumping techniques most efficiently. Failure to constantly evaluate the effects of your run on your jumping techniques is a serious mistake.

At the beginning of the run, you must accelerate as quickly as possible. Having established your running speed, you must relax and concentrate on the jumping actions. During the last four steps, you must no longer attempt to gain speed. Many beginning long jumpers fail to realize the value of jumping techniques as opposed to speed on the runway. Runway speed supplements jumping technique.

The quality of your long jump practice is important. Because of amount of hard running and the strain to which your legs are subjected during each jump, you cannot afford to practice carelessly or for long periods of time. It is advisable to alternate a hard jumping day with light running or hurdling practice. In this way, your legs are provided the opportunity to recover their normal strength and flexibility. On a day off from jumping, it is also advisable to engage in sprint work with other members of your team or group.

COUNTDOWN

Before you enter competition, or even before you practice hard jumps, ask yourself these questions to review the important fundamentals involved in long jumping.

1. Am I properly warmed-up?
2. Are my check marks properly established?
3. When I begin running, will I accelerate quickly?
4. When I arrive at the take-off, will I land with my heel first?
5. Will I execute knee lift, leg extension, and control balance following the take-off?
6. When I land, will I move forward beyond the contact point of my feet?

SAFETY PRECAUTIONS

The long jump is a physically hard event. Be sure that your landing area has been properly prepared before you attempt any jumps. Check the runway and take-off board to be sure that they are clear of loose dirt, stones, and sand. Insist on a level take-off board. As little as one-quarter inch of unevenness can result in severe damage to your feet or legs.

Wear plastic heel cups to protect your heels during the concentrated landing on the board. Maintain your spikes or shoes in good condition at all times.

Avoid hard jumping during the early phase of your training. The danger of injury is greatest when your body has not been conditioned.

CHAPTER 14

THE JAVELIN THROW

The javelin throw is one of the most complex events in the track and field program. The number of quality javelin throwers is fewer in proportion to the number of participants than quality performers in most other events. In this country, where throwing is common in our games, it would seem that javelin men should be more than plentiful. The reason they are not lies in the technique used to throw the javelin, which is entirely different from other forms of throwing.

THE GRIP

The javelin consists of three parts, a metal head or tip, a shaft, and a cord grip. The rules clearly state that the implement must be held by the cord grip when thrown. There are many variations of the grip. In all cases, the javelin is gripped with the shaft and cord grip lying in the long axis of the palm, either parallel or slightly diagonal to the fingers.

From this point on, the directions are for a right-handed performer.

Hold the javelin in a vertical position in your left hand with the metal tip pointed toward the ground. Position the javelin directly in front of your left shoulder. Reach your right hand forward so

Javelin grip, tip toward ground.

the heel of your hand is located about two-thirds of the way down the cord grip and your index finger curls diagonally around the top of the grip. Lift the javelin, and flex your right arm so as to position the javelin just above your right ear. The tip of the javelin should now be pointing straight ahead of you, and the palm of your right hand should be facing skyward. Incline the tip of the javelin slightly higher than the tail and throw it straight ahead of you to become accustomed to the feel of the grip.

A second accepted grip is obtained by positioning the javelin as before, but in the act of grasping the cord grip your middle finger is curled around the top of the grip, and your index finger is permitted to lie on a slight diagonal along the shaft. Other variations need not be considered by beginners.

It is important to hold the javelin with a firm, yet relaxed handhold. Squeezing the grip will cause the javelin to position itself across the broad axis of your palm. It is impossible to throw properly from this position.

THE BEGINNING THROW

When first throwing the javelin, it is desirable to aim at a point close at hand. Since the point will be inclined downward, there is less possibility that the implement will land on the tail and thereby cause damage.

Grip the javelin properly and position your right hand above your right ear and slightly higher than your head. Your elbow will be flexed and pointed directly ahead. Stand with both feet together. Now, with the javelin in position, step forward with your left foot, permitting your hips to move slightly ahead of your shoulders. As your weight moves forward onto your left foot, lead with your elbow, and extend your forearm up and away from your head. Direct the javelin to a point about 10 yards ahead of your position. As the javelin leaves your hand, step forward on your right foot, and stop your movement. The javelin is thrown when your weight is over your left foot. Your right foot was used to drive your weight onto your left foot. It was not part of a throwing base. The concept of throwing off your left foot must be mastered early in your training, or you will later be plagued by an inability to move your hip ahead of the javelin during the throw.

When you are able to execute the two-step throw with a reasonable degree of proficiency, it is time to lengthen your throw. Select a target some distance away from your position. The farther away the better, because this point will be used only for body position reference. Stand with both feet together. Point your toes about 10° to the right of your selected point of reference. Grip the javelin and take the proper position. Next, rotate your hips and shoulders to the rear

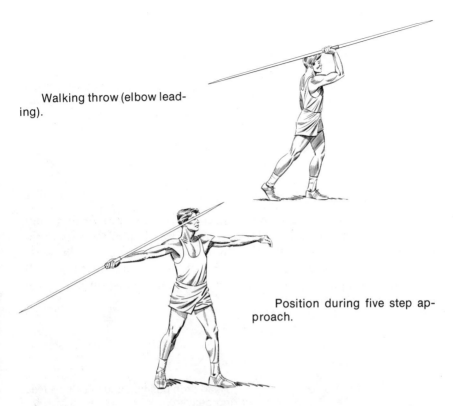

Walking throw (elbow leading).

Position during five step approach.

so your shoulders align themselves with your target and your hips are slightly ahead of your shoulders in the direction of the reference point. Extend your right arm directly to the rear, and rotate your wrist and elbow so your palm faces skyward. Begin walking toward your target while maintaining the 10° angle to the right of your foot placement. Your first step should be taken with the left foot. On the second step (with the right foot) you will notice that your feet are crossing one ahead of the other. The angular placement of your feet will permit you to maintain a position with your right hip and shoulder rotated to the rear of your left hip and shoulder. Continue to the third step with your left foot. As you take the fourth step (with the right foot) reach slightly farther forward than on any previous step. This longer step should cause your body to incline slightly to the rear. The tail of the javelin will now be inclined toward the ground while the tip is located just above your eye level and to the right of your head. As you execute your next step, place your right foot flat on the ground with your leg forming a 45° angle with the ground. Now, drive your right hip forcefully forward. Your right shoulder and arm maintain the javelin in the rearward position until your weight moves onto your left leg. Your elbow now leads directly toward your target as your forearm is directed high and away from your head. Your right palm remains in the skyward facing position during the pull through

Forty-five degree placement of lead foot and spread position of legs.

of your arm. As your arm pulls through, permit your head to fall slightly to the left side in order to provide freedom of movement toward the target. Release the javelin at the highest point of delivery. As your weight passes over your left foot, place your right foot well ahead of your body to provide a blocking action against further movement in that direction.

Head drop position and left elbow lead during delivery.

Repeat this action until it becomes natural. Then, increase the tempo of each step. Execute the first four steps with increasing tempo, followed by a rapid fifth beat. The tempo count is as follows: 1---2--3-45. The quick fourth and fifth beats represent the rapid forward movement of your right hip and shoulder and the pull through of your right arm.

Practice the five step approach until you can execute all parts with easy control. Then move back about 30 yards and introduce an approach run prior to the five step movement.

THE ADVANCED THROW

In competition, the javelin is thrown from within an area 13 feet 1.5 inches in width and 110 to 120 feet in length. Located at the end near the landing area is a foul line, over which a competitor may not pass during the act of throwing or regaining his balance.

Generally, between 80 and 120 feet of approach are used. The exact distance will depend on the length of your stride and the distance required to gain maximum controllable throwing speed. The prime purpose of the approach run is to bring the thrower to a tempo from which he can execute an efficient five step delivery.

Starting from the foul line, estimate the distance you will cover with 16 running strides along the runway. Establish a check mark by having a partner mark where your 16th stride touched the ground. Now turn about and face toward the foul line. Starting at the point marked by your partner, run 11 strides and have your partner mark that spot. Your run should begin slowly and gain momentum. At the point where stride 11 touches the ground, move the javelin to the position you have been practicing during your beginning throw routines. Now, execute the five step pattern and release the javelin. If, after you have delivered the javelin, you are not over the foul line, you need to make no immediate adjustment. If you have passed over the foul line, measure the distance and move both check marks the necessary distance back from the foul line. Your final adjustment of check marks should result in a completed throw as close to the foul line as is reasonably safe for a relaxed recovery.

Check marks are not absolute. As your approach technique improves, there will be changes in the length of your stride. As surfaces vary, so will your approach.

THE CARRYING POSITION

During the approach run, it is important that you be able to move freely. There are many possible positions in which you can carry the javelin. However, two factors will be of prime importance: First, can you run effectively? Second, can you, from your carrying position, move the javelin to the desired position for the delivery?

Three possible positions may be suggested for you: (1) Locate the javelin, with the proper grip, slightly forward of your right shoulder. The point of the javelin should be inclined toward the ground. (2) Locate the javelin slightly above your right shoulder with the tip pointed skyward about 30° from level with the ground. (3) Extend your right arm to the rear, inclined slightly toward the ground. Rest the javelin along your forearm with the tip alongside your head.

Try these positions until you are satisfied that one will provide you with the most effective run and the best potential for moving the javelin into the delivery position.

Most important in developing advanced throwing techniques will be the need to control your approach run. Too much speed will prevent your being able to execute your last five strides efficiently. Establish clearly in your mind that the first 11 steps are not used to gain excessive speed. These strides are used to bring you to your final check mark in good controlled balance with the speed needed to accelerate through the delivery of the javelin.

During the last five steps of the advanced throw, you are attempting to position your body in such a manner that your feet are travelling slightly ahead of your upper body. The manner of movement should help you maintain the javelin in the proper rearward position prior to your delivery.

During the execution of your fourth, or next to last step, it is important that you increase the length of the step in order to lower your center of gravity and produce a long throwing stride. Failure to execute a long throwing stride will make it almost impossible to establish a proper foot placement with your left leg. Your foot must be placed in advance of your center of gravity, forming an angle of 45° between the back of your leg and the ground. This positioning of your leg is called the "plant," and without it you will be unable to effectively bring about a good blocking action of the left side of your body. The blocking, or stopping, action of your left side produces the required rotational lifting action of your right side and helps move the javelin to a position high over your right ear. The action of your right arm is critical during the last five steps of the approach. As you execute the tenth step of the approach, you must draw the javelin to the rear, turn your right hip and right shoulder to the rear, and maintain this position until you establish the 45° plant of your left foot. At this moment, your right elbow must lead the javelin through. Your upper arm and forearm work in the same fashion as they would if you were driving a nail into a board located about 2 feet above your head. Your elbow precedes your forearm until it passes the line of your head; then your forearm extends rapidly up and away from your body in the direction you are trying to strike.

The action of your right arm is preceded by the action of the right hip and right shoulder, leading the throw. If this action is executed properly, your right knee and foot will turn well to the inside, producing a position wherein your right foot will drag along the ground on its outside edge.

PRACTICE SESSIONS

Because the human arm is no longer naturally conditioned by throwing activities, it must be trained and hardened to the effort required to throw the javelin. Your training process must be slow, careful, and complete, or you are likely to injure your throwing muscles.

As early as possible, you should begin throwing short distances. On short throws, it is well to have a target on the ground. The target

CORRECTION CHART

Error	Causes	Corrections
1. Tail of javelin striking ground during approach run.	a. Improper arm position.	a. Maintain arm in a position almost level with the ground at all times.
	b. Lowering rearward shoulder.	b. Rotate shoulder to the rear but do not cause it to dip or lower.
2. Low delivery of javelin.	a. Failure to place lead leg at 45° angle to the ground before throw.	a. Execute a long stride into the throwing position. Permit heel to land first during the throwing stride.
	b. Improper arm action during the delivery of the javelin.	b. Lead with your elbow. If your hand moves ahead of your elbow, you cannot attain height.
	c. Failure to keep the palm of the hand upward during throw.	c. Rotate the palm up before beginning approach and do not permit it to rotate toward the outside.
3. Javelin stalling-out during flight.	a. Pulling the elbow down during the throwing action.	a. Lift the elbow as far above your head as possible during the throwing action.
	b. Throwing at an angle too steep for the speed of your delivery.	b. Attempt to deliver all throws at an angle of 40° with the ground.
4. Lack of power in throwing action.	a. Failure to maintain right hip in a rearward position during the final steps before throw.	a. Turn hip and shoulder toward the rear during the execution of the cross-over steps.
	b. Lack of forceful knee action prior to the release.	b. Drive the right knee forward ahead of the hip and shoulder during the throwing action.
5. Excessive forward movement after the throw.	a. Improper foot placement.	a. Establish front foot at 45° angle with the ground prior to throw.

will help you concentrate on keeping the tip and tail of the javelin in proper alignment.

When your arm becomes conditioned to throwing at ground targets from 10 to 20 yards away, organize your practice into units. Each unit should be part of a progression toward a final throw. The duration of a unit will depend on the time needed to develop proper skills.

Your first unit should be concerned with throwing from the two-step movement. The range of your throw should be from 15 to 30 yards. Your prime objectives are to develop good hand and arm position during the delivery, good directional flight, and strong abdominal contraction to produce upper body rotation during the throw. Usually, when you are throwing distances in excess of 15 yards, it will be necessary to incline the tip of the javelin upward during the throw. Think of throwing into a cylinder without touching the inside. The tip of the javelin will lead and the shaft will follow directly behind it. Throw the javelin on an upward course and permit it to fall to the ground tip first. You must avoid trying to pull the tip of the javelin back toward the ground. To provide effective lift to the javelin, keep your palm directly under the javelin when throwing.

Unit two should relate to the five-step throwing action. You are now concerned with developing a rhythmic approach to the throw and improving the position of the right hip and shoulder prior to the throw. The five-step approach permits the speed required to execute the throw from the left foot plant. The speed will not be sufficient to execute a 45° plant and continue through the throw, but it will permit you to approximate this position with an effective release. During the fourth step of the movement, you must lower your center of gravity and maintain the rearward position of the right hip, shoulder, and arm. As the throw is executed, concentrate on the lead action of the throwing elbow.

Having developed an effective five-step movement, you can move to the third unit and begin using a full running approach with the javelin in the proper carrying position. During this unit, you must attempt to ascertain the most efficient running approach from which to execute the five-step movement. While speed is important, you must be able to carry into the five-step movement with rhythmic control. During this unit of practice, you can establish the placement of your approach check marks. You can also practice the varied carrying positions and establish which will permit the most effective transition into the five-step movement.

A fourth unit of practice can be reserved for development of a strong knee, hip, and shoulder action preceding the release. During this unit you must learn to establish the 45° plant of your left foot. Approach with normal running speed and emphasize the plant and abdominal contraction that provides upper body rotation into the throw. Neither good rhythm nor proper momentum can be developed without a full approach.

Concentrate on throwing with the momentum of your run. Don't attempt to make every throw a hard delivery with your arm. Most javelin men refrain from throwing more than twice each week. The number of hard throws you attempt will depend on the basic condition of your arm.

Early in the season develop speed and agility through sprinting and footwork drills. Learn to run sideways, backward, cross-step, and at a broken rhythm. Practice until no running position is uncomfortable. These drills will enhance your ability to make the required adjustments during the approach.

Throw in varied wind directions until you are completely familiar with the flight characteristics of your javelin. You can never know the conditions that may prevail at another field or on a given day. The javelin will react differently to a tail wind, a crosswind, or a head wind.

COUNTDOWN

Before you enter competition, review the factors most likely to produce your best effort by asking yourself these questions:

1. What is the condition of the approach runway?
2. Are my check marks properly located?
3. How much momentum do I need before I reach my final check mark?
4. How can I keep the javelin well back during my approach?
5. How will I establish a low center of gravity before my plant?
6. Why must I keep my hip, shoulder, and arm well back before I deliver the javelin?
7. Will I pull the javelin over my ear and head at the moment of release?

SAFETY PRECAUTIONS

When used improperly, the javelin is a dangerous implement. It should never be thrown in crowded areas, nor across areas where others are apt to travel. The weighted tip and cord grip must be kept in good condition to help provide proper control of the flight and release of the javelin. A loose tip can cause the javelin to veer off course after it has been released and a loose cord grip can make the hand slip during the release.

Proper shoes are extremely important to javelin safety. The possibility of slipping during the act of throwing must be avoided. Dry hands and a dry grip are important to controlled direction during the release, so keep a towel available at all times.

CHAPTER 15

THE POLE VAULT

In recent years, the pole vault has been one of the most controversial events in track and field. With the advent of the fiber glass or soft pole, vaulting records have improved at every level of competition. Almost overnight, high school records surpassed college records and college records moved up beyond international and world records. While the hard pole is still used to some extent in high school competition, almost all vaulters jumping 13 feet or higher now use soft poles.

A vaulting pole is a tubular device of bamboo, metal, or fiber glass. It may be of unlimited size and weight, but it may have no assisting component other than two layers of adhesive tape applied with uniform thickness. One end of the pole usually has a protective tip, and it is that end that is inserted into the vaulting box in the act of jumping.

The vaulting box in which the pole is planted is made of wood or metal and must conform to specific standards. It must be fixed in the ground in front of the vaulting pit so that its upper edges are flush with the take-off area.

The vaulting pit has a minimum dimension of 16 feet wide and 12 feet deep. The material in the pit must be high enough to provide a comfortable landing of the body in any position. The minimum height of the composition material should be 18 inches; 36 inches is preferred.

The distance between the vertical uprights may not be less than 12 feet or more than 13 feet 2.25 inches.

The pole vault cross bar must be long enough to extend beyond the supporting pins of the upright. It may be of wood, metal, or other suitable materials, and may be triangular or circular in shape.

POLE SELECTION

In the final analysis, one of the most critical factors involved in good vaulting is pole selection. Modern vaulting poles are usually given a safety rating by the manufacturer. The rating, which indicates the extreme limits of weight and/or handhold height for the user of the pole, is printed on the pole or indicated by a serial number printed on the pole. Always check the pole rating to be sure the pole will safely bear your weight.

Today, metal or fiber glass poles are most commonly used. Since the soft vaulting pole demands great care, the beginning vaulter is well advised to learn lead-up skills on a hard pole. The basic techniques of vaulting do not change because of the pole and a hard pole will probably last longer in the hands of a beginning jumper. Some coaches feel that the value of a soft pole is lost in jumps under 12 feet because the duration of time involved does not permit efficient use of the flexibility of the soft pole.

Initially, your prime consideration in pole selection will be safety. When you have mastered the lead-up skills and develop advanced techniques, you will probably wish to try many different poles in order to find the particular make or model that meets your needs. Regardless of your choice, never jump on a pole that is not right for you.

LEAD-UP SKILLS

Before you begin vaulting, a number of lead-up skills must be mastered. You must learn proper pole carry, the approach run, the plant, the take-off and swing-up, the pull-up and turn, the push-off, and the landing. All of these elements combine to produce the final effort, but they can be learned to some degree without executing a jump. Many substitute methods have been devised to help learn the skills needed for jumping and many hours of practice should be devoted to mastering the fundamentals that will finally produce your first jump.

The pole carry

From this point on, directions will be for a right-handed vaulter. Place the pole directly in front of your body with the tip of the pole on the ground and your right hand about 6 inches from the top. The upper end of the pole should be about 6 inches from your chin. Next, lower your hand to your right side so your palm is facing the ground and the pole is located in a diagonal position within your grip. Reach your left hand forward and grasp the pole, palm down, about 24 inches away from your right hand. Lift the tip of the pole off the ground and bring the tip to a point about level with your head. As you execute this movement, your left hand will become a fulcrum and shift toward the rear in order to balance the pole. Naturally, your right hand will also shift rearward as it provides the downward pressure required to hold the tip of the pole up. This is the pole carry position.

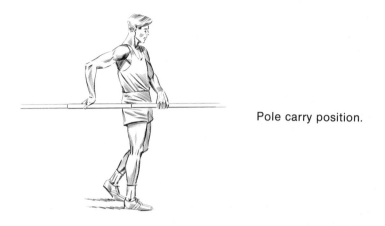

Pole carry position.

When you begin to run in this position, you must maintain the same relative position of pole and hips. The pole is pointed straight ahead and the hips are at right angles to the direction of the pole. Your shoulders are turned slightly toward the right in order to help maintain the position of the pole directly forward. Your running action should be as natural as possible while carrying the pole.

The approach run

The approach run is executed to attain the momentum required to lift the vaulter off the ground and over the cross-bar. The most desirable qualities of this movement are maximum controllable speed and exact foot placement at one or more checkmarks along the runway.

During the approach run, your speed must be controlled within limits that will permit you to execute efficiently the movements that will produce the jump. If you run too fast, you may not be able to coordinate the complex series of movements required at the take-off. If you run too slowly, you may not attain enough momentum to help lift you over the cross-bar.

Exact foot placement along the runway is required to attain the proper positioning of the pole during the plant. You may refer to the chapter on long jumping to learn how to locate and use checkmarks.

The plant

The plant is the transition movement between the run and the actual vault. It is executed by moving the pole from the carry position to a placement of the tip in the vaulting box and your right arm slightly flexed directly over your head. The movement of the pole during the plant is controlled by your right hand. It must be swung forward close

Plant position prior to take-off.

to your right hip and out to a position in advance of your head. Your left hand serves only to guide the pole in the proper direction. Your pole plant must start two strides before you leave the ground and it must be completed one stride before you leave the ground. Planting the pole early is an attribute that will produce an efficient transition from the run to the swing. When the tip of the pole strikes the vaulting box, your shoulders must be at right angles to the runway or your body will be forced too close to the pole before you leave the ground.

Learn the pole plant by first walking through the motions while concentrating on the proper movements and position of the pole. As you find the movements becoming natural, increase your speed gradually.

The pole plant is completed when your left foot leaves the ground. Prior to this, as your left foot comes in contact with the ground, your right knee must be lifted forcefully upward into the vault. This movement of your right knee assists in producing transition from horizontal movement over the ground to vertical movement upward toward the cross-bar. Without this lift, your arms would be subjected to excessive strain as your left foot moved off the ground.

When the pole plant is executed, the first significant difference between the soft and hard pole can be realized. Because the soft pole bends to a greater degree, a vaulter is able to maintain a slightly higher hand hold while approaching at the same rate of speed.

The take-off

The take-off must occur with the left foot directly under the top or right hand. You must spring off the ground with a forceful lifting action of your right knee so as to reduce the strain on your right arm and hand. Failure to produce this movement will often result in your top hand's sliding down the pole at the moment of take-off. During the take-off, it is important to permit the pole to remain ahead of your body. If your right arm has been flexed in a position above your head, your arm will absorb some of the shock of the plant and help you remain behind the pole. If your arm is extended, you will be quickly pulled forward against the pole and will lose momentum.

The swing-up

During the take-off, the second significant difference between the soft and hard pole is realized. The greater bend of the soft pole allows the initial movement of the vaulter to be relatively flat and his velocity to remain close to that established during the approach. The hard pole vaulter begins to rise almost immediately and the pull of gravity reduces his speed.

The soft pole vaulter must take advantage of the momentary flat movement by rocking back and getting his legs well up toward his hands as soon as possible. This action must take place under and behind the bent pole. The hard pole vaulter must delay any rockback action until his body has come to a position of alignment with the pole. Then he must quickly swing his legs past the pole and up toward his hands. During this movement it is important for the hard pole vaulter to remain close to the pole. He must not swing his body around the pole; he should pass as close to the pole as possible.

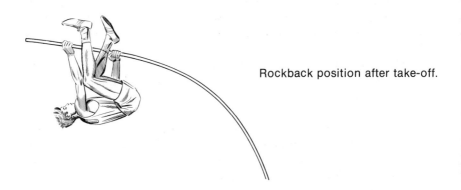

Rockback position after take-off.

The primary difference between action on the soft and hard pole occurs in the trailing leg. The soft pole vaulter must bring his trail leg up toward his hands immediately. The hard pole vaulter swings his trail leg toward the pole and, upon aligning with the pole, he brings it up toward his hands. In both cases the action of your trail leg must bring your center of gravity close to the path of the pole or you will lose momentum.

The pull-up and turn

During the pull-up and turn the third difference between the soft and hard pole becomes evident. Through the swing-up action the top of your right arm has been extended and the greater part of your weight has been supported on this arm. As the pole unbends, your pull-up begins. Your body is in a position with your knees tucked toward your chest and your feet above your head. As the pole unbends it pulls upward. You in turn must attempt to pull your body toward the pole as you extend your feet upward in the direction of the top of the pole, or above that point if your hand hold is close to the top. The energy that was stored in the pole as a result of your run, plant, and take-off will now lift you upward. As the pole completes its un-bending process, you execute the turn by twisting your hips around and away from the pole. The soft pole technique requires that you delay the twisting action of your hips until after the pull has been almost completed.

The pull-up and turn of the hard pole occur simultaneously. As your body passes to the left side of the pole, your knees are brought to the tuck position, your arms begin to pull, your legs extend, and your hips are twisted around and up toward the top of the pole. The entire action flows from movement to movement. When vaulting with a hard pole, it is important to attempt to keep your weight back against the pole during all of the pull-up and turn. In this way, your center of gravity is located close to the lifting force and less energy is required to bring your body to the highest possible point.

Pull-up position prior to turn.

The push-off

The push-off occurs at the top of the jump and is one of the most common weaknesses of beginning vaulters. As your body reaches the peak of your jump, you must push yourself away from the pole and then quickly pull your hands over the cross-bar. Many vaulters fail to execute this action efficiently, and as a result knock the bar off either with their chest as they fall back toward the ground or with their hand as they fail to pull it over the top of the bar. The action of the push-off should produce a flying away effect in relation to the cross-bar. The importance of the push-off cannot be underestimated. It is the cul-

Push-off position after turn.

mination of all that has gone before and can totally destroy an otherwise good jump. As the bar is cleared by your body and your hand loses contact with the pole, a slight lifting of your heels toward your back can produce a lifting effect in your shoulders that will assist in clearing your hands over the cross-bar.

The landing

If the landing pit is of proper construction, you can accomplish the best possible landing on the flat of your back. The pit will absorb all the shock of the landing and there will be little danger of bouncing off the surface. A landing on your feet should be avoided in a properly constructed pit because you will tend to bounce and could possibly fall out of the pit onto hard ground. If the pit is not properly constructed, don't jump.

When you have cleared the cross-bar, it is helpful to focus your eyes on some object that will help you relate to the landing pit. Look for the horizon or the cross-bar so as to establish your relative body position in the air. Do not attempt to turn toward the pit with your face or chest. Fall backward and control your position so as to avoid landing on your neck or head.

Landing position in pit.

ADVANCED TECHNIQUES

The advanced technique is a product of well-learned lead-up skills and can only be accomplished through concentrated attention to details and fundamentals.

The approach run is initiated between 100 and 130 feet from the vaulting box and must be executed so as to produce an exact foot placement at the pole plant and take-off. Speed on the runway must be controlled so as to permit efficient execution of the vaulting movements.

As you develop your vaulting skills, the height of your handhold will become a critical factor. Many beginners attempt to hold the pole too high. Generally, you should always be able to vault higher than the position of your top hand. If you are unable to accomplish this feat, it is usually because you have not learned to transfer energy from your run to the pole and you are probably in need of a lower handhold. Have a partner stand at right angles to the vaulting box and observe whether your pole is reaching a point vertical with the ground. If it is not, you are either holding too high or improperly executing the take-off. If you begin to experience difficulty in your advanced techniques, remember that a problem does not coincide with the point at which a fault occurs. Rather, it is the result of something that has occurred before. As an example, a fault that occurs in the swing-up is probably related to improper action during the take-off and may even be related to improper pole plant or run.

PRACTICE SESSIONS

Vaulting practice sessions should never begin until proper body condition has been attained. The danger of serious injury is more prevalent in the pole vault than in any other event.

When you have attained sound body condition, your first unit of vault training can be concerned with becoming familiar with the pole. Learn to grip and balance the pole. When you feel you are acquainted with it, place the tip in the vault box and swing into the pit. Then, with the help of a partner, you can attempt to duplicate a vault by having your partner hold the pole in the plant position and assist you as you swing into the pit. Your partner holds the pole and you move back on the runway three or four steps. Run toward the pole and grasp it about 8 feet from the tip. Spring upward as your partner pulls the pole toward the pit. If you coordinate the movements well, you will be able to accomplish a fair swing-up. As you become familiar with these movements, increase the height at which you grasp the pole. With a soft pole you will soon be able to produce

CORRECTION CHART

Error	Causes	Corrections
1. Late pole plant.	a. Shoulder of upper hand twisted toward rear.	a. Maintain square position of shoulders in relation to runway.
	b. Not reaching forward during pole plant.	b. Get pole into vaulting box one full step before take-off.
	c. Over-running take-off point.	c. Relax during last three strides.
2. Improper take-off.	a. Failure to lift lead knee into jump.	a. Spring upward during the take-off so as to change direction of movement.
	b. Failure to bring rear foot forward quickly.	b. Accentuate bringing rear foot forward and up immediately following take-off.
3. Poor swing-up.	a. Failure to rock back against pole.	a. See No. 2 above.
	b. Failure to transfer weight of body to top hand.	b. Attempt slightly firmer action of left arm after take-off.
4. Poor pull-up.	a. Failure to raise feet over head during swing-up.	a. Rock back hard after leaving ground.
	b. Improper timing of pull.	b. Wait until rock back is completed before pull-up starts.
5. Incomplete push-off.	a. Failure to extend arms during push-off phase of jump.	a. Drive pole down into ground during push-off. Keep pole close to your shoulder as you push-off.
6. Hitting cross-bar with hands.	a. Passive arm action during push-off.	a. Lift hands over your head after push-off.

a reasonable bend in the pole and become acquainted with the natural recoil action that will take place following the bend.

In your second unit of work, you can begin learning proper pole plant. In the initial attempts at a pole plant you should walk through the movements, concentrating on an early plant. As you gain confidence, increase the speed of your approach, but have a partner observe at what point you execute the plant. Keep your right hand close to your body as you move the pole forward and up to the take-off position. When you feel you are able to approach and plant well, attempt a few short runs, followed by a plant and take-off. Do not become concerned with the speed of your run, but concentrate on the plant and swing-up.

Lead-up skills of this nature require patience. Because all the actions occur in a very short period, it is difficult to ascertain just what factors might be disrupting your efforts. Attempt to develop a definite pattern of movements, since this will provide a constant from which improvement or correction can be made.

Your third unit can incorporate the use of a cross-bar in the jump. Place the bar about 6 feet from the ground and attempt to vault over it. Locate the cross-bar well behind the back of the vault box so as to require a definite swing-up to accomplish clearance. You can estimate the position of the bar by placing the pole in the vault box in a vertical position. Move the standards about 2 feet to the rear of the vertical pole and place the cross-bar in position. Remember that you want to spring up toward the bar while staying behind and under the pole. Most important, avoid pulling the pole back toward your body after you leave the ground.

Your fourth unit can be concerned with executing a pull-up and turn followed by a push-off and properly executed landing. Attempt to develop rhythmic movements in relation to these skills. Powerful movements will be needed later, but rhythm is more important at this stage in your program.

As your skills improve, move the bar upward, but avoid increasing the speed of your run. Learn to use the pole and proper body movements to attain height.

Practice sessions must be used to improve technique and your progression upward must be contained within your ability to execute controlled movements. There exists no value in jumping for the sake of clearing the cross-bar. Each jump must have a specific purpose planned to improve the total quality of your skills.

COUNTDOWN

When you finally enter competition, have a set plan or routine related to your jumping habits. Before you attempt your first jump, ask yourself this series of questions:

1. Are my check marks properly established?

2. What effect will the wind or weather have on my approach and jump?

3. During my plant and take-off, what factors will influence a good technical jump?

4. How can I effect a good pull-up, push-off, and turn?

5. How important will clearance on this jump be in the final results?

6. Am I holding the pole in the proper position?

SAFETY PRECAUTIONS

Safety precautions in pole vaulting are extremely important because many external factors can produce dangerous situations. Your pole must be safe for your weight. The pit must be properly arranged and cleared of any foreign material. The runway must be cleared of loose material or stones. The take-off area must be level and provide good footing. Your hands must be dry and your pole must provide a surface that will reduce slippage during the plant. In this consideration, tape can be used to help provide a more solid grip. Finally, an assistant must be present to catch the pole as it falls back from your release so as to prevent structural damage from a sharp contact with the ground or the vaulting standards.

GLOSSARY

Angle of delivery. The angle at which an implement travels in relation to the ground after being released from the hand.

Center of gravity. The point about which all parts of the body exactly balance.

Check marks. Points located along a runway to assist an athlete in attaining an exact stride pattern.

Fartlek. A method of training based on running untimed variations of pace.

Interval running. A method of training based on running continuous changes of pace over measured and timed distances.

Jogging. Running at slow cadence.

Lead leg. The first leg of a relay or the first leg to leave the ground in any jumping action.

Pace. Rate of movement while running.

Passing zone. A 20-meter distance within which the baton is exchanged during a relay race.

Pulled muscle. An injury to muscle fibers.

Reaction time. The interval between a stimulus and a voluntary response.

Repetition. A method of training based on running distances shorter than race distance at a slower pace, or faster than race speed if the distance is greatly reduced.

Sector. The area bounded by two radii and the included arc of a circle.

Stagger. Placement of starting lines in step-like fashion for the purpose of equalizing the distance run around curves by runners required to remain in their lanes during any part of a race.

Standing start. Starting from an upright position.

Starting commands. The oral commands given by the starter prior to the firing of the gun.

Starting gun. A pistol of 32 caliber, or greater, used to start races.

Starting line. A line drawn at right angles to the edge of the track from which a race is initiated.

Take-off foot. The foot from which a person leaves the ground in a jump.

Time trial. A practice run during which the participant attempts to produce a maximum effort.

BIBLIOGRAPHY

Breshahan, George T., et al.: *Track and Field Athletics*, 7th Ed. St. Louis, The C. V. Mosby Co., 1969.
    317 pages and 181 illustrations of progressive training procedures, conditioning programs, and hints on conducting track meets.
Dunaway, James O., and the Editors of Sports Illustrated: *Sports Illustrated Book of Track and Field Running Events*. Philadelphia, J. B. Lippincott Company, 1966.
    Fundamentals of sprints, hurdling, and middle and long distance running.
Dyson, Geoffrey: *The Mechanics of Athletics*. London, University of London Press, 1962.
    One of the finest books related to the mechanical principles of track and field.
Ecker, Tom: *Championship Track and Field*. Englewood Cliffs, N. J., Prentice-Hall, Inc., 1961.
    A summary of thoughts on coaching of 12 famous men who have produced great athletes.
Gordon, James A.: *Track and Field*. Boston, Allyn and Bacon Inc., 1966.
    Special training exercises for all events, illustrations, mechanical principles related to all events.
Stampfl, Franz: *Franz Stampfl on Running*. London, Herbert Jenkins, Ltd., 1955.
    Develops programs of interval training and provides year-round progressive schedules. Descriptions of great historic races. Somewhat dated but a must for any good track library.

PERIODICALS

The Journal of Technical Track and Field Athletics. Four issues per year. Contains articles by coaches and athletes related to all phases of track and field training.
Wilt, Fred: *Track Techniques*. Track and Field News, Inc., P.O. Box 296, Los Altos, Calif.

RULES AND RECORDS

Official National Collegiate Association Track and Field Guide. Phoenix, Arizona, College Athletics Publishing Service.
    A guide to rules of track and field competition and the results of most major collegiate competitions.
National Federation of State High School Athletic Associations. Track and Field Rules and Record Book. 7 South Dearborne Street, Chicago, Illinois, 60603.
    The official guide for the conduct of high school competition. Includes some records of state and national importance.